S0-BII-226

changing faces

By Tonya Nemanic

OXIDE BOOKS
Salt Lake City, Utah

First Edition

ISBN 0977042456

Text copyright © Tonya Nemanic

Cover design © Rachel Scott

Cover images © Marlene London
MarleneLondon.com

All rights reserved. No part of this publication may be reproduced or transmitted in any form or by any means, electronic or mechanical without the written permission from the publisher, except brief excerpts for the purpose of review or promotion.

This is a Juniper Press and Oxide Books product,
Published by Juniper Press

Library of Congress Cataloging-in-Publication Data

Nemanic, Tonya., - 1967 -
Changing Faces - 2007

PREFACE

This book is about love, fallibility and how vulnerable we are. If you have been hurt in love never cast it aside, never give up, never walk away. No matter where life takes us or has in store for us, love is the greatest of all the treasures.

ACKNOWLEDGMENTS

To my son, Jonathan, my father, Frank Nemanic - The Viking King, Hallard Weber, and my publisher, Mark A. Taylor - for letting me be me, enthusiastically. To Amy Babcock for yoga and facials on Sunday; to Michelle Korous for letting me be on the couch anytime; and, to Nancy Davis for inspiring me to run as fast as I can.

DEDICATION

This book is dedicated to the men I have loved and who have loved me. And, to every woman who enjoys themselves, who sees their own failings, and who loves themselves anyway.

*changing
faces*

Andrea —
You are one of life's
pleasures — always a joy !! :-)

You are Grand —
with Succulence

Jon

Chapter One

There are important moments in life where fate or destiny - whatever you choose to call it - changes everything. Something ends so something else can begin. I am enjoying a glass of Merlot and listening to a woman pour out her heart in a song.

"I wish I could fly away, bringing on a sunny day. I hear a bird fly through the sky; sometimes think I could die."

I mouth the words and close my eyes. I feel as if the words are flight itself and meant for me. I take another sip of wine, fully enjoying it flow through me. I want to be a bird and fly away.

I knew early that the dream of the big house with a white picket fence, a perfect husband and a band wagon of children was not for me. Still, I believe in fairy tales - I'm just waiting for mine to materialize from the ether.

Now, I'm on my way to the airport and moist, sad tears roll across my eyelid and down my cheeks. Damn! I won't let this happen, I protest, but it is too late. Why does this always happen? Some strange emotional up-thrust always happens when I'm on my way out of town.

The airport is packed and the crush of humanity brings me from my melancholy. Everyone is in a rush, trying to reach a destination or finding their way back home. Perhaps some are like me, searching to find *the real* home they have waited so long to know but have never seen. Scanning each person quickly as they pass by, I wait for someone to truly *see* me, to identify me as the *one* they lost; to take me by the hand and lead me home. And, if I stay alert, I might recognize someone I have never met before; someone known to the depths of my soul.

At the security line, I slip my stiletto heels off and watch the backs of people in front of me as they shift from side to side. I feel the tension of impatient, self-important people all around me, fuming at the indignity of being just another person, of standing anonymously in line, stripped of their titles and bank accounts and positions in society. Now, we are all the same, shoeless and naked to the X-rays - ready for inspection. A man nearby looks at me with a lustful glance. I nearly laugh out loud; I've always been fascinated by the difference between the outside appearance of things and their inner substance. I spread my legs slightly apart and my short skirt hikes up. I smile and he looks down and away. Just as I thought, another coward.

"Take off your shoes," the security person says.

"Do you have a laptop or computer?" Another asks.

"Take off your coat. Empty your pockets."

"Do you have your boarding pass?"

I take my clothes off one piece at a time. The young security man blushes. I'll bet he enjoys this power, demanding a slight striptease from any woman he wants.

Back on the concourse, I pass a large group sending off another Mormon missionary to ply his save-your-spirit trade in some far-off locale. There is a numbing sameness about these people that unsettles me - as if they all came from the same womb or gene-pool. One big family unit. I feel especially uncomfortable with the subservient nature of the Mormon women in my community. These Mormons are polite, pious and unassuming on the outside but filled with holier-than-thou judgments on the inside.

Knowing that I am leaving this place - the place of my birth - if only for a day, refreshes and enlivens me. I will be able to breath free air soon. The suffocating and stifling energy of this place works to undermine people at their core, and sometimes I feel it's killing me.

With each passing moment I feel better. I

suspect part of what lifts my spirit is the impending unknown. The act of leaving, of embracing the mystery, touches some unfed place deep in my soul.

I love the sound of my stiletto heels clicking on the tiled floor - like a Spanish dancer's castanets. I admit to dressing a little provocatively for this conservative city. Perhaps I'm striking a blow for freedom - pushing out the boundaries and creating more breathing space. I love short skirts, high heels, snug-tops and revealing necklines - all that naked, lustful skin. I love to watch the look on their faces - men and women alike - as they sneak a peek. When I catch them, I smile and try to make eye contact. Some look away quickly, shocked that I dared to discover them. I laugh because they act like children doing something wrong. But, in their minds, they believe I am the bad one.

Waiting to board my flight, I search the details of my past - one time period after another - not sure what I'm looking for or why. I guess I believe that our past is the basis of our future, so I sift through it all; trying to find kernels of truth so I can use them to be more in control of my present and future. Mostly, I'm trying to help myself visualize a new kind of future - based on the past but entirely new and different.

I know *things* happen for a reason - but the

question is, what is the reason? When I am on the right track, or the flow of things is right, I feel as if a hummingbird is humming. It is a sensation I look for in any event or meeting.

I am on my way back home, but I'm not feeling good about it. I'm not sure what I will find and I'm in no mood for more problems. I have a beautiful house, a business I'm feeling no passion for, and a teenager, Jonny, who is testing my limits.

Before I left he said, "I know when your mad mom, and your not there yet." This was as we drove home from the police station after he stole my car, went for a joy ride and was arrested. He acted sufficiently contrite but smiled and offered me a "care bear hug." He makes me laugh but much about being a parent to a teenager - destined to find and cross every limit - is trying.

The pilot announced we were landing in ten minutes but the problem is, that was twenty minutes ago. When the flaps open, I put my chair in an upright position and gather my things. I watched the massive Wasatch Mountains and Salt Lake Valley pass by but we do not land. We are doing a fly by. Passengers are getting nervous and starting to squirm. We bank to the left over the Great Salt Lake, then bank sharply to the right and circle - approaching the airport from the north.

"Ladies and gentleman," the pilot finally announces, "we are having a problem with our wing flaps. We decided to test them before landing, and sure enough we do have a problem."

The lady across from me gasps and grabs the arm rests. Her knuckles turn white and her face has the look of terror. I casually glance at her, and comment, "Now, that's something we didn't need to hear."

The pilot continues, "Don't worry we can still land, we just need a longer runway."

Great. I'm not in the least bit worried. I've been told by many seers and therapists that I'm going to live into my nineties. They can't all be wrong.

Touching down, we race to the opposite end of the longest runway but safely stop near its end. The woman next to me hasn't breathed since the flap announcement. Her face is ashen and looks like someone under water, holding their breath. I laugh out loud, partly because of her face, but mostly because I know it's not my time - yet.

I believe I may have finally met the man of my dreams. I know what you are thinking, but I think this time it's true. I keep telling myself - and anyone who will listen - that I don't believe in fairytales but I sure hope I'm wrong. I mean, look at reality, how many times does the fairytale relationship turn out to be crap? I admit, I've had my share of idiots and abusers and users but I can still hope, can't I? What is a girl raised in a family with a loving mother and devoted father - not to mention and a society that endlessly promotes the idea of fairytales - suppose to do? Abandon the idea completely?

Life always happens when you are least expecting it. When you aren't even looking. Arthur is a bit taller than I am and has the most amazing ocean blue eyes. His smile excites me and brings a tear of joy to my eyes. He has a hint of grey through his temples, giving him a distinguished countenance. He is charismatic and charming. He could be an actor or a TV show host.

Arthur and I met a couple of years ago. We both own salons and have a lot in common, like an endless parade of prima-donna stylists coming and going, and a long list of unhappy female clients who seems to have everything - big houses, luxury cars, lives of leisure - but only focus on what they don't have. Their husband's have provided well for them - a point they begrudgingly admit - but it doesn't matter, the husband is always the bane of their existence. While living the life of pampered queens, they complain endlessly about everything, and especially about not being with someone who is truly *special*.

When we met, Arthur was married. It was at an industry affair and shortly after I heard he was getting a divorce. From afar, it appeared as if they had everything. Sometime later, I heard he had gotten married again. I ran into him again some time later. He said, "My wife is a red head too, you know?"

I smiled and thought to myself, "She's nothing like me."

Years later, while calling salon owners to unload some product that wasn't selling, I cold-called him. We exchanged niceties and he seemed interested in what I was doing. I invited him to an event at my salon and he showed up with his front desk manager.

I was discreet but secretly stunned that he came. At the entryway, he took me into his arms and gave me a big hug. He brazenly looked at my breasts, "I didn't know you had twins!" he said laughing, "When did you get those?"

"A long time ago," I blushed. "Where have you been?"

We flirted and talked and laughed and drank wine throughout the event. He kept making goofy faces at me which I tried to one-up with my own.

Afterwards, he was off to meet some friends.

He handed me his card and said, "We should go hang out sometime."

"What about now?"

He was obviously taken aback by my invitation. For my part, I think the wine was talking - but it is important to take opportunities when they arise.

"Sure, why not."

Feeling a little embarrassed, I asked, "Did you have other plans? Am I intruding?"

"No."

I think he really meant yes.

He made a quick call to his buddies; they were at a local strip club - one of his regular haunts. He told them he had a change of plans.

We drove to a nearby local dive where he likes to sing karaoke. We drank beer and I laughed until I cried. I hadn't had that much fun in months. Several of his friends were already there and Arthur introduced me. He couldn't keep his hands off me. It was wonderful. I hadn't had a man's hands fondle me for a long time. We kissed as if our mouths had longed for this moment for an eternity. His hands caressed the twins as if he had been longing to touch them for a lifetime.

Later, he drove me back to my car. We kissed

and fondled each other in the parking lot until I asked if he wanted to go to my place. I felt like I was living a high school adventure all over again.

Then the shocker occurred.

"We have to go!" I exclaimed.

"Why?"

"They have a video camera in this parking lot for security. We're being video taped."

"That would be cool."

It really wasn't cool. My parents owned the buildings and parking lot!

Eventually, we made it to my house, climbed into bed and immediately passed out.

The next morning I woke, screamed and jumped out of bed. It wasn't because I found a strange man in my bed but because I had over slept and was late for work. I ran to the bathroom and jumped in the shower. Arthur dressed and peeked into the shower. He gave me a kiss, " I guess I'll talk to you later."

That was a year ago now and what I didn't know was that Arthur was going to change my life - again. I hadn't had a relationship like this in years. I had grown accustomed to being alone. It was easier for me to just put up walls and keep myself stable and distant. It was more convenient that way, I didn't have to take risks or expend the energy to get to know someone.

Chapter Two
Back at the Airport

Entering the cabin of the plane, I depart my life here and rejoin my spirit, my astral journey. Flying away is a metaphor for just that, flying away.

I see all my past relationships in a new order when I'm afforded some physical and psychic distance. Over the years, I have made mistakes and missteps, violating my own personal code time and again. There are many intersections in life and few of us pick the right path the first time around. Like most of us, my personal code was developed when I was young, earnest and callow. While it has served me well, it has been ill-fitting and inhumane at times, too.

Essentially, when it came to relationships, my personal code assisted me in finding and maintaining a relationship that possessed all the things I liked about marriage but without the negative drawbacks. I wanted an exclusive, intimate pairing with a partner who was my friend, companion, confidant and lover. Someone who, for better or worse, would stand by me when life's uncertainties arrived; and, someone I could be there for when they needed me. I wanted to build a secure future that included a home where we could gather as a family and be at peace. A place to come back to when our adventures were over and take refuge in when trials and tribulations came knocking. A relationship that would prevail and be everlasting - at least for this lifetime. How naïve I was!

I realize my code was pieced-together when I was young and very romantic. I watched my parents and admired them for what they portrayed; and, I based my code on the carefree life they made for me and my sisters as children. It was a wonderful fairytale and I was part of it; most of it was true but now as an adult, I realize some of it was not as it seemed. It was the traditional family: a father who worked and was strong and kind, a mother who stayed at home and took care of us, making sure we were loved and protected; a neighborhood where we could play safely - never giving a thought that something bad could happening. It was America in the 1960s, the America before Vietnam, drugs, free love, the Women's Movement and now our mindless consumerism.

Now, as I'm being transported high into the weightless world of clouds and dreams, on my way to some *other* place, I can sit back and try to decipher what happened and where I failed to live up to my promise and where the code *itself* was unrealistic and unable to withstand reality.

Let me say their names out loud: Tom,
The Pilot, Mister Teeny-Weeny, Mr. Cabin M
Mr. New York, and now, Arthur. I have loved them
all, each for different reasons but all in an attempt to
capture or fulfill my fairytale dream. I have had many
learning experiences, but despite this I have made the
same mistakes again and again. Perhaps it was meant
to be. Perhaps they are not mistakes. Perhaps, we must
risk and fail, and risk and fail before we are finally
rewarded.

In-between these men I have loved were others,
many others; minor players in my grand education and
three-ringed circus-love life. Oh my, what have I done?

I think of Tom and *our* first love. If we are
lucky, each of us has a first love in life, a first taste of
our growing out of childhood and into being an adult.
If we are really lucky, the ending of our first love affair
is gentle and not too traumatic.

First love is sanctioned and beloved by society
but I realize now, it is seldom about real love and
more about idealistic dreams about love. Tom sired
my beloved son, Jonny, and he will always - for
better or worse - be his father. Not knowing how real
relationships work, Tom and I played house. It was a
costly lesson and one that each subsequent generation
of loving parents holds their breath about, hoping it

won't go too badly for their child.

Tom, for all his continued problems in taking responsibility and learning how to work for a living, might have been more grown up than I was when we were together. I thought we would be together forever and we would live happily ever after. He taught me my first devastating lesson: nothing lasts forever. I remember clearly how he stood sideways across the living room, extending his arm and pointing a finger told me, "Tonya, you need to grow up! You need to let go of the fairytale!"

I thought, how dare you! If it is a fairytale I'm protecting, then it is my fairytale to do with as I see fit. So - be off! Tom wasn't the man I thought he was; always running away from problems, being angry and out of control. He was boy in man's clothing. My mistake was I was in love an idea of who he was, but not who he really was. My Prince Charming was a commoner who was lazy at heart and couldn't stand on his own two feet - without his momma. He didn't take care of his princess, rather he wanted his princess to be his momma, too. In a fit of rage, Tom ripped out a giant plug of my hair and I knew it was time to move on and release the power I'd gifted him. When he left, I felt I was dying inside. I dragged around for months, unable to find joy or satisfaction in anything.

With Brad, I was damaged goods. An unmarried mother who deserved to be punished. And, punish me he did. Not so much intentionally but because Brad was a loser. He was a liar and deceiver and thief and a two-timer. I lowered my head and went along because I felt worthless. No one would want someone like me. Someone who has forsaken her code and dream. Someone entirely unlovable. Ultimately, Brad's true nature came to the fore and I began a quest to find the Magnificent Self I had somehow lost. I was on a bigger mission, that of motherhood and of making sure my son had every advantage the world could offer.

Then came The Pilot, the older man who had everything and seemed so together. I was his trophy and he treated me that way. He showed me off and polished me up and set me on the mantel and wanted me to be and do whatever he wanted. Wear this, not that. Do this, not that. Don't say this, say that - or shut up. It was the illusion of the perfect relationship with the big house on the hill. The successful man and his beautiful younger companion. The impeccable exterior and the hidden interior - the numbing superficiality. Image and illusion is everything.

Mister Teeny-Weeny was in the same category and the nickname speaks for itself. Not much else to say about that. It was what it was. Another man looking for the perfect woman to have on his arm but with little or no real love, sharing or intimacy.

Two different men, with the same lesson for me to learn. Did I need a man with money? I would make my own.

Then, Mr. Cabin man. I loved the idea of him. He was everything I wanted and more. The comfort I felt in his arms was something every woman longs for - dreams about. He was the one. He loved all of me and meant it. He was kind and sympathetic and tender. He taught me to enjoy romance and showed me what it was like to be treated like the most important person on the planet. I had kissed a lot of frogs but then I kissed a real prince. He gave real hugs and real kisses. He will always have a special place within me. I will always love the gift of loving me that he gave throughout the years. He was simply amazing, always a romantic. The fatal flaws: he was afraid of my son - and fearful of being committed again. He wanted me and not a family. I can't blame him really.

What a heartache, to have found someone truly special and not have it work out. He loved me and I loved him - but it was not to be. No happily ever after - just a long-term, part-time love affair that took place in a romantic secret cabin surrounded by the magnificent Wasatch Mountain Range. Oh, how I longed for that man, and secretly, still do. But I am much older and more experienced now. Reality arrived at the doorstep of my little girl fairytale land. Knock, knock. Who's there?

Mr. New York will always be a little boy and nothing more. I was caught up in the illusion of grandeur, blinded by the stars and his over-the-top New York lifestyle - one based on borrowed money and broken promises. I should have listened to my son, Jonny. Just because someone dresses nicely and takes you to exclusive restaurants, it doesn't mean that they are all they profess to be. It was a hot air dream. Once the air started seeping out, it deflated into a heap. I learned to love myself from him and to be aware of the illusion of grandeur.

Now Arthur. Well . . . this one is all about me. A mirror image of myself. I am what I am, and he lets me be me. He is a romantic, a manly man; always kissing and teasing as if we are kids. Something of a Peter Pan really. Always disappearing to Never-Never Land and finding new adventures. With Arthur, I remind myself, "Go with the flow." That's all I can do. He is mine but he wants to leave, to escape this stifling, backward, religious homeland.

Arthur does not belong here. He can't breathe in this place. It is not home. His comments and complaints do not go unheard - even if I do not respond. I hear what he is saying - too well. But, what I hear and what I see are two different things.

Fairytales can make the world go round. Mine has given me hope and much to ponder. I still hold out that one day it will be my turn, yet the men I love come and go. Why does love not last?

Chapter Three
A Fairytale Beginning

It was one of those magical childhood winter days. A big storm had blown in over night and left our rural neighborhood covered with a mantle of deep, luxurious snow. The pine trees lining our long driveway stood like sentinels, stately guardians watching over this fairyland where all the bushes and plants were transformed into giant hump-backed animals. Everything was fresh and new and I couldn't wait to get out into it. I remember clearly standing in my nightgown in the living room and watching my dad dressed in his overcoat clearing the driveway and walk. It was mid December and I was seven-years-old. I can close my eyes and see it right now.

Perhaps the thing I remember most vividly was the silence. It was as if the storm had brought peace to the entire world. Little did I know that before darkness fell my life would be changed - forever.

By late afternoon I joined my older friend, Kathy, sleigh-riding down a neighbor's driveway. The house stood at the top of a hill and the driveway arced down to the right and then entered the little-used roadway. It was the best sleigh riding day in history. Time and again we raced down the hill and my new sleigh cut through the snow like a knife. I floated on a soft cushion of white. I cared little about the cold and as night fell it really didn't matter. We were the Queens of this wintry Utah day.

Kathy told me it was time to quit but I begged her for one more ride. We would go down together. I laid on my sleigh while she pushed us faster and faster then jumped atop of me and off we went - riding double-decker. Down the drive, faster and faster and then out onto the icy street and nearly all the way to the four-way stop sign several empty fields away. It was a record-breaking distance! We laughed and screamed and hollered the entire way.

From this point on my memory becomes sketchy. All I remember is I was on the sleigh and she was pulling me back up the road. I saw headlights coming up behind us then . . . POOF! Nothing.

The next thing I knew a neighbor was standing over me crying hysterically. People told me later I was crying and screaming but I do not remember any of it. I do, however, remember trying to get my legs to move but nothing happened. I couldn't feel anything below my waist. The pain was unbearable and I can feel it right now, all these years later.

I kept pleading, "Unbury my legs. My legs are buried. Get the snow off of them. They won't work, unbury them!"

The next thing I recall was my mother pushing the neighbor - the woman driving the car who ran over me - aside and kneeling down beside me. She was beautiful and I felt safe. I remember her screaming at the neighbor but at the time I was oblivious to it. I told myself to move my legs but nothing happened. I looked down and they were twisted - backwards. I couldn't believe it - where are my feet, I screamed! All I could see was the back of my snow boots. I tried to move them again but still nothing happened. I don't recall being afraid but with all the commotion - everyone in the neighborhood standing in a circle around me and then the ambulance ride to the hospital - it was a dream.

I learned much later that the neighbor had had an argument with her husband and was racing to get away from the house when she hit us. According to her, she swerved to avoid a giant block of ice but plowed into us instead. Luckily, Kathy was thrown clear but the car rolled over me. Once she realized she had hit something instead of stopping and finding out what it was, she put the car in reverse and backed up to see what it was. The result was, she ran over me again.

At the hospital, it was all lights and action. People running this way, then that way. They cut my pants off and I heard voices discussing what they should do. I felt pain - deep pain. I heard a drill and then . . . nothing.

I was in a state of bliss. I had no idea where I was or why I was there. It was calm and serene and I felt at peace. Floating. Voices coming closer then fading into silence. Light. Darkness.

For the next two weeks, I remained in a deep coma. My mother never left my bedside, except once every day or two when her brother took over while she went home to cook for the rest of the family, bathe and change clothes.

"She's waking up! She's waking up!" I heard my uncle's voice proclaim. He was calling out to my mother. I heard her rush across the floor to my bedside. Suddenly, there she was, smiling and crying simultaneously. At first I didn't know where I was or what happened to me but I soon found I was imprisoned by traction and needles in my arms. I was unable to move. Over the next few days, I learned what had happened to me. By the time they got to the hospital I had nearly bled to death. They frantically replaced five pints of blood and my hip bones were broken and one femur had been pushed all the way into my abdomen. They had to remove it from my cervix. They inserted large shiny mental pins that protruded from my knees and were connected to ropes with weights attached to keep my legs straight.

What amazed and disappointed me more than anything was how much time had elapsed. I missed Christmas. I couldn't believe it! I was devastated - but not for long. The good news was that Santa hadn't forgotten me. In came a wagon filled with all my Christmas goodies.

Over the next weeks, I had many visitors including the neighbor who ran over me. She cried and cried and expressed her sorrow. I forgave her but I was to learn later that she had not forgiven herself. As a child you do not understand everything and I couldn't quite understand why if I could forgive her, she could not forgive herself.

Then, more bad news. My mother told me that my best friend, Curt, had been in a bad accident. For a moment, I was excited, thinking he might occupy the bed next to mine, but that was not to be.

"Curt didn't make it," my mother said, holding back tears. I remember feeling empty and unable to think. Just like me, Curt had been sleigh riding moments before the accident. It could have been me. I could be dead. He had accepted a ride home after sleigh riding in his uncle's truck when it got stuck on the railroad tracks just a block from home. His uncle got out to see what was going on when a train smashed into the car from behind, killing them both. To this day, I can still see Curt's face, his eyes, smile and I sometimes hear his voice floating on the wind at dusk.

Over the years, I have often thought about Curt. What would he have been like had he not died? Why him and not me? The death of someone close to us changes us in some subtle - almost undetectable - way. I'm convinced that when it happens to us, especially in childhood, the river of our soul changes course.

Six weeks later, I was released from the hospital but I was not free. Before I left the doctors put me in a complete body cast. I remember thinking the body cast was cool, too. So did my siblings and friends. When our car pulled into the driveway, I was greeted by everyone in the neighborhood. My Viking dad, I call him that because he is big, strong and wears an enormous handlebar moustache, opened the garage and there against a wall were five brand new Red Rider sleds. I don't know what ever happened to those sleds, but I've never gone sleigh riding again.

Dad made me a cart out of a grocery shopping cart so I could get around. He cut the top off and bolted a piece of plywood to it with a thick cushion and covered it with fabric. It was a hit! I loved it and everyone wanted to ride on it. Since I couldn't roll over in my body cast, I spent a lot of time pulling myself around, laying face down. At age seven and just out of the hospital, I was in heaven.

Every day a private teacher from school came to the house and made me do my lessons. After six months, the doctors cut away the cast and used pliers to pull the remainder of the pins from my knees. It was excruciating and I tried not to cry but could not stop the tears. I was glad no one told me in advance what the plan was.

While free of the cast and pins I still couldn't move. I was stiff from not moving and my muscles had atrophied. I couldn't bend at the waist or stand on my legs. My feet and knees were weak and didn't want to move. We left the doctor's office with a pair of crutches and instructions about limbering me up and making me strong again. It took another month for the pain to go away and I before could put weight on my legs again.

One thing I hadn't expected about my accident was I became the center of attraction. My Viking dad built my first bedroom in our unfinished basement. It was the envy of my sisters. That first night in my very own bedroom was unforgettable. I had a new bed, chest of drawers and got to pick the carpet and paint. Now, I had my own place where I could be alone. I spent many wonderful hours by my self playing and thinking about my life and wondering where it might take me. I felt extremely lucky - as if God had shined a light on me - because I wasn't dead like Curt or in a wheelchair like other kids who were in car accidents.

I felt safe and at peace. I was part of a family that loved me. A family with a mother who did not work outside of the home but who worked very hard raising us kids, and a father who was strong and patient and who loved us. I remember how tired he was when he came home from work all dirty and greasy after a long day. He would wink at me and tell me I was *his* girl. We were a family - a true family - that loved each other and lived just to be together. It was a simple time back then, before our world evolved into something quite different and far less caring. Today, when I think about true love and men and family, my mind always goes back to that time. Too our little family and sleigh riding on that magical wintry day.

Every day I did my exercises and used my crutches. I became quite accomplished, going up and down the stairs with ease but soon I wanted to get back on my own two feet. One day alone in my room I decided to chuck my crutches and walk. I was determined to get back on my feet again. I slide off my bed, touched my feet to the floor then very tentatively stood up on my wobbly legs. My goal was to walk to the dresser, just two steps away. I felt shaky and unable to balance. I could hardly carry my own weight. I took one step and then another. I shouted, "Mom! Mom! Come!"

She bolted down the stairs, thinking I had hurt myself.

"Look!" I screamed, "I'm walking!"

"What?" she said, nervously.

"Watch this." I moved away from the bed and walk towards her. It was like a toddler taking its first tentative steps.

The expression on her face was priceless. Then, just like my mother, as I moved closer, she stepped further back.

"Mother!" I shouted, fearful I would fall, "Don't!"

She smiled, then laughed and we both erupted in cheers. I nearly fell over with joy but somehow kept my balance. I was finally back! I could walk again.

A few weeks later I returned to school where I was the center of attention again. I received special treatment from everyone. I got to leave class early to get to the lunch room and to be the first one on the bus. Soon, my celebrity faded and I was just another kid like everyone else. After nearly one full year I was finally back together again.

Chapter Four

"What are you doing?" I asked Arthur.

"Kicking back."

It's Wednesday night and Arthur and I are finally able to talk.

"Since I've never asked, where do you live anyway?"

"I'm just up the road and down a few lights."

The only time he has been to my house was a few weeks ago and we were both so drunk he passed out just as we were going to *do it*.

"Care if I come over?"

"Sure. I'd love it!"

I was already in my car and rounding the corner out of my cul de sac. I'm wearing pink pajamas with knicker bottoms and fuzzy tiger slippers. They keep slipping off the brake pedal of my new jaguar. My bottle of wine and a few necessities sit on the seat next to me.

He is waiting on the doorstep. Jumping out with my slippers on my feet and the wine bottle and purse in my arms, he broke out into laughter - like there was a big joke.

"Is it so bad?" I ask, feeling a little embarrassed.

He cups his hands over his eyes and continues

to laugh so hard he can't speak.

"Look at me!" I demand.

"No, I can't," he says in-between laughs. "It's too funny."

I pummel him with my empty hand but I guess he's got a point. Isn't it wonderful when you can truly be yourself from the beginning of a relationship? It usually takes months before we show all our warts or are able to break wind in the presence of our newly beloved. With Arthur, we skipped all the phony formalities and can just be who we truly are.

On his comfortable couch we pick up where we left off the other night in our drunken passion play.

Arthur goes for the *twins*, caressing them and running his hands everywhere under my pajamas. It feels wonderful to have a man I am crazy about touching and caressing me so tenderly. This time, no one is going to pass out. I let my hand slip down across his stomach and into his shorts. Oh, my . . . no Mister Teeny Wennie here!

We take each other's clothes off and he caresses my body gently but with more and more passion. We are more aggressive and I get on top of him, needing to find relief for the aching between my thighs. I have one orgasm after another and he is not even inside me.

Stop, I suddenly tell myself. You have to stop,

Tonya!

"What?" he asks.

"I'm not on anything right now. No protection!"

"It's okay," he says, having difficulty reigning
in his passion.

"What do you mean, it's okay?"

"Don't worry about it!" He pulls me back on
top of him.

Now I'm concerned. "I've heard that before.
Men always say . . ."

"No," he interrupts, "I've been fixed, snipped!"

"What do you mean?"

"I can't have kids. Vasectomy."

I surrender and we make love first on the couch,
then out on the patio table under the stars. Oh, the
starry sky has a whole new meaning - and then in his
bed.

Later, he tells me about his divorces - two of
them - and how the second wife left him more bruised
than the first. His first marriage was about love and
lasted twelve years. He was on top of the world, his
business was thriving and they were the envy of family
and friends. A big house on a hill, nice cars and plenty
of money. At the same time, he was miserable. 'I
couldn't figure it out,' he told me, 'We had everything
but when I was alone I had to face the truth, I just

wasn't happy. It really wasn't her; I was just really unhappy!'

One day he woke up and without warning told his wife he wanted a divorce. It was amicable, but they had to sell their dream house and business (they were partners) and went their separate ways. Luckily, they didn't have any children.

A client lined him up with his second wife. She was a red head who bleached her hair blonde and had a two-year-old son. Apparently, he lost his better judgment - perhaps it was the great sex and his loneliness - but he asked her to marry him and she accepted.

Arthur knew something was terribly wrong when on their honeymoon cruise he caught his new bride giving her phone number and cabin room to the ship's captain. A few days later, she mysteriously disappeared for a few hours when they were docked in an exotic port. He is convinced she snuck off to have sex with the captain.

"Why didn't you get the marriage annulled as soon as you got back?" I asked, incredulous.

"Stupid, I guess," he looked away and continued, "I couldn't face the truth. Have you ever been there before? The truth is right before your eyes and you can't accept it . . . not until later, when it's too late."

I knew what he was talking about. We are all able to swallow the most ridiculous lies and betrayals when we love someone and the truth doesn't match our dream of what should be happening. Self delusional behavior.

"She loved me treating her like a princess," he told me, smiling. "I would have done anything for her. She didn't want to work, so I told her she didn't have too. She wanted to buy something, I got it for her. She saw a car she wanted, I went out and bought it."

Having taken care of myself for so many years, it all sounded too good. I would really like to try that lifestyle sometime. It would be interesting to have someone take care of me rather than the other way around. I probably wouldn't like it, but hey, I'd like someone to offer to make me a princess.

Soon, it was evident she didn't love Arthur and was just in it for the free ride. He packed his bags and left the house he purchased before they met. She stayed on with her son and new boyfriend.

"You mean," I asked, "your ex stayed in the house you owned and brought her boyfriend there?"

"Yeah, she was screwing him all along but she got a lawyer and I was out!"

No wonder men are so apprehensive about new

relationships. If I had been him and it was my house, the courts would have kicked his butt out in an instant. But, if you are a woman with a child, well you can be a total slut and the guy can be an upstanding citizen and he gets the boot. Ah motherhood, it has some unfair advantages.

"I had to pay the mortgage and stay away from *my* house for a year until the courts ordered her out."

Arthur does not have a problem telling me about his past relationships. While many men have difficulty communicating with women, Arthur is an exception. I have longed for a partner who I don't have to quiz or submit twenty-questions to before I could find out what's going on in their head! He is wonderful . . . I think.

Strange, but when I want to talk about the future, Arthur is less forthcoming. One thing I do know, he doesn't want the same experiences he had in the past happening again. I'm certainly not out for his money, I make my own. I don't believe in having affairs when in a committed relationship. It is important, of course, to have great sex though! The power of the penis does matter.

Over the next few months, we have endless conversations about his ex-wives. I arrived at a point where I just didn't want to hear about them any longer.

Enough already! I know you were miserable, I tell him, but now you are with someone else, someone who won't do any of those things. I don't think he is listening because in his head he is reliving - moment by moment - the anguishing incidents he was forced to endure.

We all have a sorted past. In part, it makes up who we are now and what we think. I know I am a product of my past and I also know it is my duty to not make the same mistakes again.

Chapter Five
At Twenty-Two Everything Seems Possible

Friday night and I'm driving my new convertible sports car to Karen's apartment to start another weekend adventure. I'm still stinging from my mother's comment as I headed out the door, "Where do you think you are going with your butt hanging out?" Despite this, or because of it, my life seems filled with magic. My red hair dances in the wind and the promise of the azure blue sky lifts my spirit. Pressing down on the accelerator and turning the stereo volume higher, I hold-on; I feel as if I am in control of everything, the road, my life, my destiny.

What is it with my mother, anyway? One minute she is proud of me, the next she looks at me like I'm some cheap whore.

Of course, my butt isn't hanging out! I'm just a fashion girl with the body of an aspiring actress. A small skirt for a small ass! My god, I'm twenty-two-years old, what do you expect?

I'm five-foot-eight inches tall, one-hundred and twenty pounds of endless leg and long natural red hair. People say I should be a model; and, I wear stilettos as if they are part of me. I'm ready to party, to get down, to got to the top, to conquer the world! Isn't that the way it's suppose to be? You know it is!

Have you ever felt as if you had been somewhere before but didn't know the outcome? That's how I feel tonight - as if I have some hidden adventures deep in my memory of all this - especially tonight - and the act of doing it, is a replay.

I find Karen sitting on the counter in the bathroom with her feet in the sink. Her house stinks of cigarettes and the stereo is blasting. She is applying makeup like a doctor performing some life or death surgery.

The phone rings.

"Don't answer it!" she screams.

"I wasn't going too!"

Ring . . . ring . . . ring.

"It's probably that jerk . . . you know . . . what's his name . . . Kevin."

"You mean, the short muscleman you slept with last week?"

"No, that was Jacob. Don't you remember anything? He's history. Kevin's the one I was with last night. He was a good lay but once you get past the smile, he's a dope."

"I guess I can't keep track. Why'd you have sex with him if he's such a dope?"

"Don't be so rude! Why shouldn't I? I didn't

know he was an idiot until Christine told me. Anyway, he's just using me. He just broke up with his girlfriend!"

"You weren't using him?"

"Stop it, Tonya! Don't make me laugh."

Once upon a time not long ago, a sweeter Karen was madly in love with "the love of her life" until she discovered he was cheating on her. Now, she seems determined to break hearts and prove her own worth by having sex with as many boys and men as possible.

"How many does that make . . . a hundred or two, more?"

"Stop it! You heard me! You're so crude!" She turned away from the mirror long enough to scrunch her face at me before turning back.

"What does it matter anyway? Men like me and I like to have fun."

"Whatever."

It's true. Men do like Karen. Petite, beautiful, great body and soon to be very rich. Wherever we go, we are the center of attraction. Everyone stares, old people, kids, men and women. After a while, I don't really notice anymore - until, that is, they stop looking. I love Karen but wonder what is going to happen to her. Is she going to grow up and be one of those women with the dream house and dream man - one that will do what it takes to support a family?

It's not going to happen for me, I can already tell. I'm far too independent, too successful and . . . . well, I don't want a man telling me what to do, what to wear and how to do my hair!

Tragedy seems to follow Karen. Her mother committed suicide when she was a little girl and she never knew her father. He was a one-night stand, a drug addict who disappeared long before she was born. Like her mother, Karen has a keen eye for losers and bad boys. You know, handsome and troubled, usually momma's boys. Talented, sometimes musicians, always high on something. They all have the big, enormous, grandiose dreams of rock-n-roll heaven. Romantics. Fatalists. Artists. Needy little boys looking for a woman to sleep with them, then be their momma - and give them money.

Karen was raised by her grandparents who were already old when she was a child. They died when she was in high school and now, in a couple months, when she turns twenty-one, she will get a million dollars from their estate. Tragedy and affluence - a combination worthy of a book.

We toast the new night with a couple of beers and decide to start our weekend drama at a local watering hole where we can both see and be seen.

Drama seems to be of paramount importance when you are in your early twenties; too bad it always includes pain. It revolves around boys and girls that have finally arrived at adulthood and don't know yet what to do with it. Not old enough to see the wisdom of leaving their past behind or see any future in the future. Live for today because tomorrow we shall die. It should be the anthem of our twenties.

From one bar to the next, stopping in-between at two parties. It played out just as I had seen in my premonition: boys and girls drinking, saying stupid stuff, hanging on to someone else's boyfriend or girlfriend, and jockeying to have sex with someone they shouldn't be with. Sex, trauma and drama. Fun and games.

I drove and Karen drank. We had a pact, one designated drinker and one designated driver. The entire night I couldn't stop thinking about Tom, my eight-year on-again, off-again boyfriend. He and I got into an argument earlier and I couldn't shake my negative thoughts. I didn't tell Karen what I was thinking because I already knew her response: Tom is a jerk, a user and abuser.

Earlier, Tom showed up at my place and described in vivid and lustful detail a beautiful blonde with big boobs who was hitting on him at the local swimming pool.

"She was so fine," he said, with relish. "Tight little butt with blue eyes and tits hanging out of her tiny bikini."

"Why are you telling me this?" I asked.

"What? Why are you getting so uptight? You asked."

"I asked about how the pool was!"

"I'm just telling you what happened. You don't have to get so defensive."

"How would you like it if I told you about all the boys who say stuff to me?"

"Who says stuff? What stuff?"

"Nobody. Really! Nothing! I was just trying to make you see how I feel."

"You want me to tell you what I did and then you blame me for it! I can't win."

"I just don't need you telling me about other girls and how hot they are. You're almost drooling."

"I'm outa here. Why don't you go take a valium or a midol . . . whatever you guys take during your period?"

Why does Tom always have to bring up other girls? Aren't I enough for him? What does he want me to do? I think he wants me to know there are others out there who want him - that are better for him. Of course, it just feeds my insecurities. I always want to look and be my best.

When I say Tom is my boyfriend, it is part illusion. When we first started seeing each other I had such romantic little-girlie ideas. How naïve I was eight-years-ago at fifteen-years-old. Tom is my first love. Back then, I was convinced I would marry the first man I slept with, that we would have a slew of beautiful kids, and he would take care of me like my Viking father did my mother.

Tom and I met at the the Frost Top Drive-in, on main street. He was seeing a friend of mine at the time but started coming on to me. After she got over losing him to me, she told me they had sex every day and that he had "a good one." I didn't understand what she meant, but now I do.

A week or two later, on the Fourth of July, Tom showed up on my doorstep. He asked if I wanted to ride up into the canyon and then go watch the fireworks. It was a wonderful, dreamy time - but the fireworks never seemed to end. Throughout high school, it was one thing or another, one adolescent drama scene after another. He was angry, jealous, possessive and childish. I was insecure, clingy and would have done anything to make him happy. I was swimming in a pool of women's hormones and my emotions about love and life were all confused with my dreams of forever and always.

I always felt as if I were Tom's secret girlfriend. I'm not sure why, maybe it was my appearance. His mom always wanted him to be with a blonde. She was a bottle blonde herself. Perhaps she was worried about having red-headed grandchildren. I was not interested in having children and certainly didn't want to trap someone into marrying me. There were other reasons I wanted to spend time with Tom. He was sweet and handsome and even thoughtful sometimes. I still don't understand why he wanted to keep our relationship a secret. Wasn't he proud of me?

It was some time in my early teens that I started to have dreams of future events. I would dream something, then a week or two later - it would happen. In the case of Tom, I think my intuition was trying to tell me something. I remember in one dream I was driving to Karen's in my new sports car and after filling up at a gas station, I saw Tom drive by with a cute blonde sitting next to him. I just shook my head and drove away. Sure enough, a week later, the dream turned into reality.

After dropping Karen back at her apartment to await the most recent Prince Charming she met tonight and invited over for some fun, I drove by Tom's house.

When I confronted him about the blonde in his car, he told me she really liked him and that is why he took her for a drive.

"If I went out with every guy that liked me," I said, "you would never see me again."

He couldn't believe it. "Sure," he said, "with all that red hair you should feel lucky to have one boyfriend."

I was speechless.

Over the next few weeks, I invited him to some local parties and he noticed all the attention I received. Men seemed enamored with me, red hair and all. It was as if he wasn't even there. I had to tell people I had come with my boyfriend and then introduce him. I think he finally got the message, and realized how lucky he was. I think some men feel it important to have other men want what they have.

So, for the last eight years, that has been the way it has gone. Is this the way all relationships are? A few years ago, I really thought it would work, but I'm finished now. Back then, he even admitted he loved me. I heard that when a man tells you he loves you, he really does - since men would never say such a thing unless it was true. I had been drinking and having a good time with some friends when he told me. I was so shocked and happy I cried for days. I knew his pronouncement didn't mean marriage, but I also knew my life was somehow change.

He moved in to a bachelor pad with some friends. Karen managed to hook up with one of the roommates to add to her list. She and I would go out and do our usual weekend routine and end up at the bachelor pad later. It was one of those prolonged good times in our troubled relationship periods. We all acted happy and let the good times role.

After Christmas, Tom's little brother was killed in an automobile accident and in some fundamental way it changed him. He was handsome, had a great body and wanted to be a doctor, then a pilot and then an entrepreneur - whatever field or profession his mother's current boss or boyfriend was involved in. But after his little brother's death, he was lost and commented many times that he wished it had been him who died rather than his brother.

Since I had just turned twenty-one and was all grown up, we decide the best thing - for him and me - was we should find an apartment move in together. It was time to do it right. Coming from a family with two failed marriages, and in the middle of a deep depression, Tom was reluctant, but I was happy as I had ever been. He said he loved me and I loved him. What else did we need?

At first, everything was wonderful. We shared the work, the fun and all the expenses. We went to parties and never left each other's side. I always thought it was the way relationships should be. We were best friends and lovers. Our souls resonated. Why would anyone in a relationship fight and be distant? I couldn't imagine it.

We had an amazing time together. I finally felt as if my world was turning around. I had what I thought was the perfect home life. My career was finally taking off big-time and I couldn't have been happier. It was as if *my* fairytale dream was going to come true. I was actually starting to hum. It was as if bliss was at my fingertips. Could life get any better than this?

Tom worked out of town in construction the first year we lived together. I flew to Las Vegas or drove a few times to see him. We talked about moving there. I checked the job market and even talked to a few employers. Even though my career was starting to take off I was willing to pull up roots and start over again. After all, isn't that what a relationship is all about? A balance of each other's needs, priorities and time? A give and take? After a few trips, he decided the timing wasn't right.

Ultimately, he had found work with a local

welding company. Outwardly, he seemed happy and content. It was good to have him home again. It was while doing construction on a local amusement park's water slide that he told me about the real cute little blonde girl in the bikini he met.

Because he told me that he "loved me" I had nothing to worry about. Everybody looks, don't they? Even though I felt insecure, I decided to not let it get to me and I forgot about the entire matter - well I mostly forgot. About the same time, his best friend became engaged to a woman he had only known for a few months. Tom and I had now been together as a happy couple for one year.

At the wedding party for Tom's friend, I got the shock of my young life. The moment I saw the little blonde with blue eyes in the reception line, I knew it was over for Tom and I. I was to be replaced. She was looking right passed me as if I were not even there, focusing her stare on Tom. I turned quickly to Tom and he was standing there flatfooted looking back at her. His face was flushed and he was gaga - entranced. I melted into the background, I did not exist anymore.

A fog fell over me. I looked at her, then at him. My intuition was letting me know. Not long after the wedding everything started to change.

I wondered then if I had seen in-between

worlds. Be still my mind, I kept thinking.

At first, I didn't want to believe it was over, so I fought or denied its existence. But, all the signs were there. I didn't want to see or listen. The wedding was in October and by the end of November we spent Thanksgiving at separate locations. Tom went to his mothers, and I went to my parent's house. It was awkward. We all know the feeling when something isn't working but we can't quite put our finger on it yet. I felt as if something wasn't right, but where should I put my finger?

Christmas, New Year's Eve and Valentine's Day came and went and while we still shared the same apartment and put up the pretense of being a couple, we were like robots who were only there physically, but not emotionally or romantically. I did my best to block it out, denying the reality of what was happening. Tom spent less and less time home; he often called to say he had to work late. In my heart, I knew what was going on.

In March, our lease was about to expire. He was the signer on the lease and I paid the utilities and groceries. When I brought the lease up, he looked to the ground and informed me he was moving back to his mother's house.

"So, does this mean our relationship is over?" I

lamely enquired. "What does this mean?"

"I don't know."

"What does it mean, you don't know?"

Tom just stood there looking at his feet and shrugging his shoulders.

I turned and walked away. I heard the door close and he was gone. I quickly got my things together and moved out.

I hate to sound like some naive dumb girl but at the time I thought we could work it out; it was something to deal with instead of running from. Was I delusional? Or, is love some kind of fucked up dream we trick ourselves into believing?

The ending of my relationship with Tom resulted in my first experience with the divorce diet. I soon had that "tits on a stick" look. Even though we were not married, I felt that living together was an equal commitment. I lost ten pounds in one week over the end of my first-love and the emotional roller coaster with a man - or a boy - who didn't know what he wanted and couldn't say what he meant.

Soon, I moved into my very own one bedroom apartment. I started the next phase of my romantic journey. The apartment was always clean when I came home. Cooking dinner for myself was fun. Men seemed to notice me more, or was it that I was now single, thin and started to notice them? Whatever the case, was I about to have some fun.

Chapter Six
Pregnancy

After the split with Tom and finding my own wonderful apartment, I met Kirk a newly divorced career man. He was thirty-four, 12 years my senior. Kirk was sharp, good looking, ambitious and on a fast track to success. Very smooth. At first, I thought he knew everything but soon found out he really knew very little - especially about women.

In every conventional way, Kirk swept me off my feet. We traveled, frequented the best restaurants and went to famous night spots. He was a real gentleman, genuine and seemingly caring. He wore expensive suits and had a great education; and, he knew what to say and when. In comparison, Tom was a country bumpkin, fresh from falling off a turnip truck with a vocabulary of grunts, groans and postures.

One day Kirk showed up at my shop.

"I have something for you," he told me with a smile.

"What?" I asked excitedly, in my most adoring voice.

He handed me an envelope that contained round trip tickets to Paris. "Can you get away from work long enough for a two week trip?" he asked.

At the time, my client list was skyrocketing and I was making more money than most men in mid-career. I didn't know how to respond. I was totally thrilled but instead of saying yes, I lamented, "But, I don't even have a passport."

"No problem," he said, smiling. "We will get you one."

He took me into his arms and kissed me. At the same time, his hands explored my ass.

Europe! I'm going to Europe, I repeated to myself until it sound plausible. Europe. Since childhood, I have been fascinated by castles and walled-cities and history and the idea of Paris. Romance. Love. Cobblestones.

A few days later, the trip was history. I didn't even make it to the passport office. When his ex-wife learned of our plans, she decided it was a good time for their seven-year-old son to spend more time with his dad; wouldn't a trip to Europe be a great bonding experience for father and son?

In the meantime, Tom showed up at my new wonderful apartment. He informed me that leaving me was the biggest mistake he had ever made. Duh!

I fell into his arms. I couldn't believe what I was doing. My body was moving forward while my better judgment was backing away. He was just so sad and so sorry. Pity fuck time. Not a smart move. We tore off each others clothes and did it on the floor. I wanted to give him what he wanted - but the question is, why?

After sex, while sitting on couch dressing, he asked if he could move in.

"No," I answered, flatly. "You cannot move in." His arrogance brought me back to my senses. "This is not going to work," I said without thinking. "Every time life shits on you, you turn to me. Nope. Not this time. That was then, this is now."

Tom couldn't believe it and went emotional. He hollered and demanded and ultimately begged. "Please," he asked, "living at my folks house is a nightmare, I need a place to stay. I love you, don't you know that? I've always loved you."

"You should have thought that earlier."

When he finally realized I was not going for it, he asked if we could do it just one more time.

Pity fuck number two.

Then, he was gone. So long Tomboy.

If a man ever tells you that leaving you was the biggest mistake ever, run like hell - never let him back in the door. If you do, you'll turn into a floor mat. He'll wipe his dirty feet on you as he comes in and as he goes out.

I had some fun with a few other men that first amazing summer after Tom. Kirk returned from Europe with his son and I saw him on an occasion or two. We never had sex though. One night while perusing his extensive library - something I always love doing - I pulled out a book on reproduction. As we sat together turning the pages, I felt butterflies in my stomach.

A week or so later, I realized I hadn't had a period in more than a month. I chalked it up to the emotional turmoil I had experienced with Tomboy and Kirk. After getting a blood test that turned up negative I felt better. When my period still hadn't started a week later, a co-worker told me that blood tests are often wrong, so I went back to the hospital and had another test.

Positive! Pregnant.

I was shocked . . . but thrilled . . . I think.

A girl I worked with got pregnant a month earlier and opted for an abortion. She offered to take me. I said no thank you and went my way. Being pregnant brings so many emotions and fears; I was so awash with conflicting feelings I couldn't think straight. I wanted the baby but every time I thought about marrying Tom I felt as if I were going to throw-up. It was the pity fuck that did it, the stupid pity fuck.

What was I thinking? I guess I wasn't really thinking. In my fantasy world I thought my first baby would be planned out; the product of a happy relationship and a decision made by two loving people. Boy, was I wrong.

Next time I was with Kirk I mentioned the reproduction book and the butterfly feeling in my stomach. I told him I was pregnant. He knew he wasn't the father but without hesitation he offered to pay for an abortion. "Do you have any idea what this will do to your cute little body?"

This was Kirk's real idea of responsibility, manhood and his view of women.

The real question was, should I tell Tom, the love of my life, or keep quiet? The bottom line was, Tom is the father and needs to know, so I invited him to my apartment to tell him the news.

"Why the hell didn't you tell me you were pregnant?" He blurted out, coming through the door.

"What? How do you know?"

"Guess? Aaron. You know, my best friend!"

"Oh . . ." I mumbled. Before talking to Tom, I decided to run the entire matter by his best friend. I was hoping he might offer clues as to how Tom might respond. I should have known better.

"How would you like to find out you got

someone pregnant from your best friend? It was my right to know first!" The veins in his neck bulged out.

"What do you mean, *someone*?"

"You want to get married, don't you?" he asked, cock-sure.

I was speechless, shocked and humiliated.

"Well . . . ?" he demanded. "Do you or don't you?"

"No, not really."

"What do you mean, not really! You get yourself pregnant and you say I'm *its* father and you don't want to get married? Bullshit! It's the right goddamned thing to do! The honorable thing."

"It may be the right thing to do, but Tom, you haven't even asked how I'm doing. Don't you even care?"

He stopped ranting and stood in the middle of the living room with his arms crossed.

"You don't want this baby Tom and you know it. It may be the right thing according to you, but . . ."

"You've ruined my future," he interrupted, acting as if he might cry. "It'll probably be retarded!"

"Retarded!"

"All those god-damned birth control pills and everything else you supposedly did to make sure you wouldn't get pregnant!"

"It's always about you, isn't it? What's going to happen to poor Tom. Grow up! Whether you like it or not, you are half responsible. You could have kept it in your pants! If the baby is retarded, it's because you are a moron!"

"Right. . . right. I see it now, you bitch!" He rushed toward me as if he were going to hit me. "It's coming clear to me. " He paced back and forth. "You did all of this . . . everything - slept with me, got yourself pregnant, went to my best friend, told him before you told me. . . all so you could get back at me for being with the blonde, right?"

"No, not right . . . I just found out and . . . I didn't get pregnant on purpose . . . I thought you said you loved me."

"Fuck that! You did this because you wanted to trap me . . . put the screws to me . . . You'll be a horrible mother, Tonya. Everyone knows it . . . That poor baby will have a horrible life . . . All because you have to have the upper hand, you have to be in control . . . you couldn't stand it when I moved out . . ."

"That's not true, Tom. I just . . . "

"You just wanted to get me away from the blonde, right? Just so you know, I'm back with her again. She is the one I really want, not you! You just want to ruin that for me. "

"I'm going to have this baby on my own! I'm not telling anyone you are the father." The words came out but I felt frightened by them. "On the birth certificate, where it says the father's name, I'm leaving it blank!"

For three ugly hours it went back and forth, one allegation then another, one insult heaped atop the last, one mean-spirited attack after another. Round after round - repeating every insult, every allegation - screaming and shouting.

To him, it was as if I had made up some grand conspiracy - culminating in me getting pregnant - just to totally fuck his life over. Never mind the situation I faced, never mind the baby inside me. Never mind who was going to pay for it. Never mind that a baby needs both a mother and a father. Never mind talking it out like adults, never mind trying to figure this mess out together.

When Tom walked out the front door and I locked it I promised myself I would never let him in again. I kept that promise to - until the next time.

The next day my eyes were swollen nearly shut, my voice had a croak in it and I was back on the emotional roller coaster weight loss program.

The words *I Love You* are an illusion. They have no meaning. Anyone can say them to anyone else at any point and it's all meaningless - it's something to say to get what you want. When someone truly loves you, it's unconditional. It doesn't need to be said as much as it needs to be shown.

A month later, I woke in the middle of the night and rushed to the refrigerator. Ice cream and refried beans. Wonderful. A few days later it was jelly beans and cool whip. At lunch with friends, someone ordered a steak and when I got a whiff of it I nearly hurled. It was the same feeling I had at an all night party after doing shots of yagermiester.

Kirk was still coming around but he decided he could no longer see me because, according to him, pregnant women are too sexy and if he wasn't going to get any, he had to stay away. With each passing week, I got larger and larger. I really think Kirk was worried that he would be viewed as the father and was not ready for that.

My doctor told me I had three choices. I could go through with the pregnancy and keep the baby. I could place it for adoption, he knew of many good couples who would love a beautiful healthy baby. Or, choice number three, which he said, "We won't talk about."

Okay.

I was in my own little big world. Micro-mini skirts, tight mid-drift tops, stiletto heels, popped out stomach. What did I care anyway? I made a point of not saying anything to anyone. It was fairly obvious by the third month but if anyone wanted to know the particulars, they would have to ask. And many did. Some were hurt that I hadn't told them. Others just looked at my stomach and then at me as if I were from outer space - and they were right - I was.

About the same time, I decided it was time to tell my parents. I didn't know what they would say or how they would take it so I put it off as long as possible.

"Mom," I said after she answered the phone, "I need to tell you something."

"What? How much money do you need?"

"No, mother it is something else. Are you sitting down?"

"Yes. Are you alright?"

"Yes, mother. I am pregnant."

"Oh that. Your sister already told me."

"What?"

Months earlier after the knock down drag out fight with Tom, I told my younger sister the entire story and like all good siblings, she ran as fast as she could to tell mother.

"Well," my mother said, spacing her words, "I hope the sex you had is worth the hell you're going to go through!"

Silence.

"I know one thing," she went on, "We can't tell your dad."

Inspiration from mother herself.

Aren't parents wonderful? They raise us to be forthright and honest and when we arrive at adulthood, all equipped to do the right thing, we find out they do as much bullshitting and deceiving as anyone.

A day or two later, the phone rang.

"Tonya, it's your dad."

"Dad. Hi!"

"How are you doing? I just thought I'd give you a call and see how my girl is."

Dad never calls any of us. For him to make a call out of the blue is laughable.

"How about lunch today?"

"Okay, daddy."

He never calls or asks any of us out.

At his shop, I find him at the wash basin, scrubbing his hands and arms. I suddenly feel famished, as if I might faint. I need to eat and eat soon!

"So," he says wiping his hands and turning to face me, "Your mother tells me you are going to make me a grandpa."

Tears flooded my eyes. I felt as if I might faint.

"I don't guess you know this but your mother was pregnant when we got married."

"Oh daddy!" I rushed to him and threw my arms around his neck.

"These things happen," he said gently. "everything will be alright."

That was it. I had dreaded this moment of face to face truth for months and in less than one minute it was said, acknowledged and dealt with, no screaming, no lecturing, nothing. Boy, do I love that Viking dad of mine.

I saw no reason to stop dating so I didn't. I had several blind dates who, when they got a first look at me, had to take a second longer take. There I was, all dressed up in a short skirt, high heels and a tight top with my stomach sticking out there a mile. Beautiful. What did I care? For the first time in my life nothing else mattered. I was pregnant and had many things on my mind.

Things like how am I going to afford this little adventure? Who would I hire for daycare? How much fudge can I eat? Do I get the whole pan and can I have more? What is this going to cost? I had become accustomed to pleasing myself, doing what I wanted and when I wanted to do it. Was all that going to change? I suspected so.

The holidays came and went and it was Valentines. I was now seven months along. I found flowers at my doorstep, more specifically, two flowers with a card. It read: "One for each of you." There was no signature but I knew who sent them, the love of my life - Tom. I sent them back.

By the time the spring flowers were popping out I was huge and ready to explode. Fifteen pounds in two weeks, seven in another. Dad shook his head in disbelief, "My god Tonya, you are the largest pregnant woman I've ever seen!" My mother pounced on him, but he didn't get it. "What," he asked, "did I say something wrong?"

"What's a girl to do?" I asked, shoveling down another taco in two bites. The chips were stupendous. How about a piece of meat loaf? At the clinic, a woman carrying twins struck up a conversation, "You are having twins or triplets?" She asked, sweetly. "Neither," I answered, smiling.

At the salon, my client list was the only thing growing faster than my belly. I felt good but after a long day my last client arrived with her mother and she took one look at me and commented, "We'll come back another time, you are obviously in labor."

Laughing, I answered, "No way, I'm not due for two weeks." After they left, I felt weak and drove to mother's house. With one motherly look, she knew my time was coming.

"Get your bag, we need to leave now!" she demanded.

"Bag? What do you mean?"

"It's time!" she shouted, running from one room to another, dressing and trying to find the car keys. She dialed dad, "Come home, it's time!" she hollered.

"Time for what?"

"What do you think, idiot? Tonya's in labor!"

I'm sure Dad thought mother was feeling frisky and wanted to go to a hotel for some fun. He would be there in a minute! In the meantime, I gathered up some old clothes I left at their house and then mother and I waited for Dad. We waited and waited until I was convinced mother was going to need a doctor herself.

"We can't wait any longer!" she told me, "lets go!"

I wasn't in any pain and strangely fell into a laughing fit. As mother craned to see over the steering wheel racing down the street and I couldn't stop finding the humor in the entire situation, we past my Viking Dad as he raced home. We pulled over when we spotted him but he just kept going. Back at the house, we found him leisurely making a snack in the microwave.

"What are you doing?" mother shouted.

"Getting something to eat, what does it look like?"

"Are you coming or not?"

"I guess if we can't wait until my burrito is finished."

"Dad!" I pleaded through tears of laughter.

"Okay, dolly."

As soon as my doctor saw me coming down the hallway, he ushered me into a room. Luckily, he was already there and had just delivered another baby.

"You are close," he said nervously, "Lets get you started!" He lifted what I thought was a darning needle, a long metal object about ten inches long, and examined it.

"What are you going to do with that?" I asked. But by the time the words left my lips, he inserted it into the place of no return.

Gush! A rush of warm water flooded my legs and the bed. The contractions really started to hurt. After awhile, I had to order dad out of the room, he was wearing a hole in my forehead where he was stroking it. He was getting freaky and my sense of humor had disappeared. For a period of time, I'm not sure how long, I was totally out of it. Then, it was over and I had the most beautiful and special baby boy in the world.

Dad disappeared to a beer joint a block away and came back just as Jonny was delivered. Dad carried an extra beer in his pant's pocket - just in case, he told us. He followed the doctor who delivered my baby out into the hallway and tipped him a hundred dollar bill. My mother narrowed her eyes, shifted from bun to bun, and scowled at him.

Two weeks later, I was back at work. I was on top of the world but now I had to support two of us and no matter how much money I made it was never enough - having a family is expensive. My client list just kept growing and growing and I was working 50 plus hour work weeks. I have always made my own money and never asked for help. I would do whatever was necessary to give Jonny and I everything we ever wanted. And, I did.

Chapter Seven
Dating

Some men see single mothers with careers and want to save them. The question is, save them from what? From being able to make decisions for themselves; from building a good solid financial future; from all the other *bad men* who might want to take advantage of them?

After Jonny was born and we settled into being a sweet little family and I went back to work full time - overtime really - and started dating again.

Kirk showed up and over a quick drink after work told me he disappeared when I was pregnant because, according to him, "Pregnant women really turn me on. I mean, I really didn't think I could keep my hands off you, so I thought it best to back off."

I wanted to slap his face. Instead, I sat quietly, sipped my wine and stared blankly at him. As he spoke, I realized I would never really forgive him for trying to convince me to get an abortion.

Then there was Tim. He was older and safe. He had recently divorced and had two small children. I never felt excited or romantic or attracted to Tim but I did feel safe. Safety is something women secretly long for; we want someone who will be there for us no matter what - especially after we've been hurt. I should have let him know that it just wasn't going to happen for us, but at the time, I was interested in the company, the free food and the movies.

I enjoyed the dating game and had rules about date night. It was all about what was convenient for me. If I needed a babysitter, who was going to pay for it? I did, of course, but if they offered I thought it was quite gentlemanly. Looking back, I was really having a great time and enjoying the independence that making good money and being young and single offers. Men were interested in me and I liked it.

During this fun-loving period, I started dating Bradley. Like many men, Brad had recently separated from his live-in girlfriend who was the mother of his two-year-old daughter. Brad was good looking and had that bad-boy confidence, something many women can't seem to resist. I found out later the bad-boy stuff was really immaturity, arrogance and a sense of unrealistic entitlement. He acted like everyone owed him something. Of course, I didn't see it coming - although the clues were clearly visible - until it was too late.

Brad was a year older than me and content with his dead-end job and where it was leading. This should have been enough to alert me something was wrong but I was twenty-three and had few tools for identifying losers. He was living the single life with some bachelor friends and doing his share of partying. He had dated some interesting women and wasn't quite sure where he fit in.

"I've had a lot of girlfriends," he told me one night after a few beers. "I mean, I've had sex with a lot of women. Forty or fifty maybe, something like that."

He paused and looked at me, trying to gauge my response, then continued, "Maybe I shouldn't tell you this, but Amy's best friend kept coming on to me so I slept with her, too." Amy was his last girlfriend's best friend. If I were to offer men some advice it would be never tell a woman how many other women you slept with or fucked over. You are just setting yourself up for failure. We are not impressed and it doesn't make us want you more.

Early in our relationship, I realized Brad always seemed to be short of cash. He liked to party and wore nice clothes and drove a respectable car but he never had any money. At the same time, my client list was getting larger and larger, and I was working six days a week, and making excellent money.

One night at a local club, he ordered drinks for everyone. We were having a great time dancing and talking and listening to music and were joined by a few friends and acquaintances. When the bill came, he grabbed it, studied it and then slapped me on the back and hollered over the music, "This is for you."

I was mortified.

A week or two later, I went out to a movie with Tim. Since Brad and I weren't exclusive yet, and he was working afternoons I saw nothing wrong with it. After Tim dropped me at my place and the moment I opened the door, the telephone rang.

"Hey Tonya, it's me!"

"Hi, Brad. What's going on?"

"I got off early and thought I'd come by."

"Well, okay," I replied. I was tired but what is a girl to do? "Come on over."

Before I could put the phone down, my doorbell rang. It was Brad.

"That was fast," I said, greeting him with a hug.

"Yeah," he said narrowing his eyes and looking at me as if I had done something wrong, "I was getting gas at the station across the street when I called."

I immediately knew Brad was spying on me. He watched Tim walk me from his car to the front door. From that moment forward, Brad changed his vocabulary and started using the "we" word to describe our relationship. When we went out with friends or happened to see someone, he always let them know we were a couple. At the same time, he started to enquire about how much money I made, and complained about how his child support left him broke all the time.

With summer coming to an end, Brad's roommates at the bachelor's pad were moving in with their girlfriends or getting married. Standing in my living room he announced that since he was already at my place all the time anyway, it would be easier if he moved in with me.

The warning signs were flashing red as I sped by them on my way to my next major mistake. He just wouldn't let me say no. For every objection I had, he had a lame answer. If he didn't move into my place he would have to move into his father's house all the way across town. We wouldn't be able to see each other as often. I wanted to stand my ground and sent him to his dad's house but I didn't. Within a month, my house became *his* house and I was transformed into his servant, sex-mate and financier. Dinner? Why of course, Brad let me run in as fast as I can and make something delicious . . . No matter that I just came home from 12 hours working my ass off or that I haven't even said hello to Jonny yet. No clean clothes, no problem Brad . . . I'll stay up late and get everything washed and ironed. Not enough money, oh my dear, we can't have that Brad, will twenty do? No. Okay honey. Here's a hundred.

What's wrong with me anyway, I kept asking myself?

Brad was generous though. One day I came home and found he had bought me a beautiful, original oil painting. He knew I loved art and found something I really did like. I was thrilled - for a minute.

"I saw this," he told me, "and knew you would love it."

I didn't know how to respond. This was the first time Brad had given me a real gift.

"Shawn and I were out driving around and I spotted this at an artist's booth. Isn't it beautiful?"

"Yes," I said, "I like it a lot."

Brad's friend Shawn was sitting nearby on the couch. He was shifting around and I felt something was wrong.

Brad finally piped up, "Yeah, when I saw this I knew you would love it but I didn't have any money with me so Shawn loaned it to me. Can you pay him back?"

I was dumbfounded - or may be just dumb. I couldn't believe this was happening. Shawn was embarrassed but Brad acted as if my money was his. In his own convoluted way, Brad truly believed he was being generous and thoughtful.

Wise up, Tonya! my inner voice sounded the

alarm. No matter how much money I made, Brad figured out a way to spend it on himself. He was using me up, emotionally, financially and sexually. Unfortunately, while I should have benefited from the sex I soon lost all my desire for him and making love became just another way I could make his life better. Climb on, climb off.

According to Brad, one of the best things about moving into my place was his daughter was able to come over and play with my son, Jonny. In fact, his daughter spent more time at my house than she did at her own. If I wasn't cooking or cleaning, I was paying the bills. He contributed exactly zero. If you are out there reading this Bradley, you are a bloodsucking jerk.

One day on returning from a long hard day at work, I found the county sheriff's at my house. I had been burglarized; someone kicked down the door and ransacked my house. Strangely, the only thing missing was Brad's expensive home entertainment center. I was very frightened and felt violated. How could this have happened to me? My beautiful sanctuary, the place I could go and be safe, had been contaminated. I sat on the front steps and cried. After the police left Brad grabbed the phone and called my insurance company.

Within a week, all his stuff was replaced with top of the line equipment. Brad knew exactly what to say and how to work the system so he ended up better off than he started. I discovered a year or two later, after finally getting him out, that he had done the burglary himself. He kicked in my door and robbed me of my peace of mind.

Have you ever seen the faces of people on television news who have suffered some tragedy or trauma like a hurricane or earthquake? They look all spaced out as if they are zombies. That is what I looked like. I was so involved in my clients and trying to make enough money to stuff into Bradley's endless hole; and, at the same time be a good mother to Jonny, I was missing in action, unable to see what was really happening to me.

About this same time, I decided to open my own salon. Although a slave and zombie in my own home, I was finding great success at work. Every week I put money away and over a period created a good-sized nest egg. I researched locations and studied small business practices and principles. I purchased slightly used equipment, opened vendor accounts with product suppliers and signed a lease on a wonderful space. I placed ads for stylists and had many referrals for great people. I did have to borrow a small amount to get the salon off the ground but I paid it back as soon as possible.

The more motivation and drive I had to be successful, the less motivation and drive Brad had. The bigger my success, the bigger his loser quotient became. As he saw my business come together and watched the money rolling in - with hard work - the lazier he became.

One evening after a particularly long and trying day, I arrived home to find a delivery truck from an electronics store sitting in the driveway. I slowed to see two men carrying a brand new giant TV screen into the house. His mother's car sat at the curb. I immediately knew what was going on. Brad had decided we needed a new TV in the family room. I drove to a convenience store, bought a six pack and sack of potato chip went to my friends, Brett and Jean's house.

Brett and Jean offered me a safe haven and we discussed what to do about loser-Brad and my unhappy situation. At midnight, I pulled into my driveway. I went straight to my bedroom. Brad was sitting in the family room with *our* fabulous new play toy waiting for me. I didn't even look at him and just closed my door and went to bed. He knew why I wasn't talking and the next day the delivery truck retrieved the purchase.

At my parent's house, my Viking dad brought home the money and my mother cooked, cleaned and took care of us kids. For a while, he held down three jobs so we would have what we needed. What happened to those days? I was convinced they were part of our American past and I would never find someone to marry me or who actually cared enough to want to take care of me. What were the chances of me and Jonny finding someone who would be willing to have us?

I finally figured out where Brad was coming from when he and I were at his father's house for a mid-summer barbeque. I was helping Brad's father's girlfriend make a salad when I overheard a father and son conversation.

"All you have to do is give a woman great sex and you'll never have to work, son."

Brad tilted back in his lawn chair and smiled his approval.

I couldn't take it any longer. Sticking my head out the back screen door, I remarked, "I don't think so!"

They just smirked and went right on as if I did not exist. The girl friend's face had misery written all over it. As for the great sex, well, that was really never the case. It had been mediocre from the beginning.

I knew this could not go on but with a demanding business and Brad's never ending needs, I slipped into the fog for several more months.

One night late I heard noises outside our bedroom window. Someone was trying to break in. I jumped up and dialed 911. Help arrived a few minutes later and they nabbed the culprit. It was a blast from Brad's past. A girl he had been seeing before we met and who accused him of fathering her daughter decided to break-in. She was drunk and furious. Sitting at the curb was her broken down sports car with a babysitter and her three-year-old daughter inside.

The police told me she came by to drop the three-year-old off with Brad. She claimed the child was his but he denied it.

Please, when is this going to end? I stood at the living room window, arms folded tightly across my chest, as the police searched the car, interviewed the babysitter - she was just being taken home when the crazy woman decided the time was right to confront Brad - and the police tried to talk sense into the drunken mother.

Eventually, I was shocked to see the police let the woman go. The parents of the babysitter arrived to retrieve their daughter and the father drove the drunk and her baby home in the sports car. I had had enough.

"Why did you let her go?" I demanded of the police officer.

"Well," he said, "she is a single mom and I thought it best."

"She was trying to break into my house! It is the middle of the night. She scared me and my son nearly to death."

"I know," he muttered, "But . . ."

"But what! She was trespassing. She was driving drunk. I can't believe this!"

The entire time, Brad skulked around the perimeter like the skunk he is. The next day, I filed a report against the police officer. He was reprimanded but nothing ever came of it. Everyone told me the same sob story: she is a poor single mother without much help and so we let her go. Well, hey! I'm a single mother too - one who has never had any help - so what about me? What about people taking responsibility for their actions? What about the police holding people responsible for their actions? I guess I should have made a conscious decision to be irresponsible myself - perhaps then I could get some help.

Brad was a boy and not a man. He didn't want a girl friend, he needed another mother, someone to take care of him, and in my case, someone to have sex with. I was just a young mother who was trying to do the best thing for my son and to find that illusive - storybook - relationship. I had always been led to believe it was waiting for me.

It took another year to get Brad out. I stopped all his purchases with my money and refused to buy him anything including birthday and Christmas presents. I did, however, buy him a sack of chocolates for Christmas.

At his employer's Christmas party I arrived late because of work and was seated next to him at a circular table. I noticed a blonde across from us glancing at him with that little girl flirtatious look. She was, of course, a bottle blonde. She thought he was unattainable and magnificent - it was written all over her face. I knew she would be the next better thing for Brad and I immediately felt lighter. I smiled at her and nodded my head.

Later, I asked Brad about her, "Where was her boyfriend?"

"She doesn't have one," he answered, acting distracted.

I couldn't help but laugh and grin. He just looked at me as if I was wacko. I was the happiest I'd been in a long time.

Brad moved out on January 2, and I couldn't have been more pleased. The long nightmare was finally over. He emptied the house of everything while I was at work but that mattered little - it was just material stuff. The only problem was Jonny had grown really attached to Brad. It was easy to understand because they were both just little boys. Jonny was devastated; he had never had a real daddy and I felt guilty.

When Jonny asked why Brad took all our stuff, I explained that it was just material stuff that could be replaced. We had each other and that was all we really needed to be happy. A week or so later when Brad stopped by for something, Jonny looked him in the eye and said, "We're going to have everything just same - even better. It just takes time, because my mother said so." He then turned to me and we smiled.

Jonny and I have never seen Brad since and I am thankful for it.

Chapter Eight
Arthur and Christopher

Arthur has taken the big plunge. He has officially moved into my house. Strange as that might seem, it feels quite natural and normal. To him, it's more complicated. He has always been married when he lived with someone. Not only was he married, they moved into his house, not the other way around.

He came home today and felt out of place, "What happened to my life?" he asked, solemnly. "Not only am I living with my girlfriend, I don't know where my life is going anymore. " His voice carries sweet melancholy.

Autumn has arrived and the leaves are turning. The mornings are cold and the days brisk. The wind blows and I ask myself, "Where will I be in a year from now?"

Sometimes I try to stop myself from thinking and just feel myself breathe. The scenarios and madness can be so overwhelming I feel I might burst. Everything is coming so quickly, all the hustle and bustle of life. I feel as if people are pawing at me. Everyone wants something. I have to stop the pawing! Where do I go to stop the pawing?

I told myself for years I wouldn't have a man

live with me again. Twice was enough and I learned valuable lessons. But, this is different. I sure hope so, anyway. Now, I have someone to help me with Jonny. I just wish I had the time to do it myself. It would be nice to pick him up from school and stop at the grocery store for something wholesome and then make dinner. Wow! A home cooked meal.

What are the chances? Have times changed so much I don't have an opportunity to be a real mom? Is it me, or has something happened in our world?

I guess it started in the 1970s with the woman's liberation movement. Well, we got what we wanted. Now we make as much or more money than men, we have the freedoms of men, and now we have a multitude of choices - and problems. Too many choices, I suspect. Most of us now long for something more simple and basic, something that resembles what our mother's had, a house and kids and no job and a loving husband who is committed to taking care of us. Lame? Could be.

The idea of being a mother sounds sweeter today. As a young woman, I hated the way the word sounded - mother. I was going to be much more than a mother and housewife and servant to some egocentric man-child. I couldn't see myself picking up stinking socks and changing dirty diapers. But, I'm changing my tune, at least for right now. Motherhood. I feel as if this *higher calling* is instilled in my sole.

Today, women see their lives unfolding in a multitude of ways. We think: I might be able to do it all! I have slowly begun to feel my passion reignite. I am excited about my future, again.

I always knew the past would play a big part in my future. The roles change and then change again. Now, after being alone for years, I slip into a new adventure with someone by my side. I have something - someone - to trust and be loyal too. I have chills thinking about being together. I even love it when he is away.

Will he cheat on me? Yes, if I think he will. Will he miss me? Yes, if I think he will. Will my business fail? Yes, if I think it will. Am I beautiful? Yes, if I think I am. It's amazing how our thoughts control or direct our destiny. I am what I think I am. I have what I think I have. I feel what I think I will feel. I have thoughts that can control the future. Change your thoughts and change your stars.

All of my experiences have awakened the spirit in me. Gandhi said it best, "We must be the change we wish to see in the world."

I need to let go of the past and live in today. I'm trying. Should I have gotten an abortion? Should

I have married Tom? Should I have married Brad? Should I have stayed working for someone else? Should I have pursued the interesting men who hoped to take me away? Should I have left this place I so dislike for some other homeland? So many questions about the past. I need to quiet those voices and be here now.

I now realize I've shut down my intuition again. It's funny but we only know something is happening inside us when it is nearly over. I am opening up again and it makes me realize I was shut down. I didn't even know it. When did it stop and why did it start again? I am paying attention to the coincidences in my life and my inner voices again.

When I'm truly open, I ask people directly what they want from me or what the real issue is. I know I've touched a button by their response. Some have a look of shock, others smile and see that I am healthy and approachable. I am convinced we all have the answers to the questions we are asking. We just need to stop and listen.

When I take time out, my mind returns to the solitude I had as a child laying on the back of my horse, Christopher. The sky and clouds above, my protector below. Not a care in the world. If I close my eyes I am back there again. I can smell the grass in the fields next to the house, I can hear my sisters voices playing under the trees, I can sense the strength and gentleness of my sweet horse, Christopher. It was during this time that clear light truth was so very easy for me to see and understand.

Somehow, after my sleigh riding accident I had a different or perhaps deeper perception of people than before. I spent many childhood seasons alone avoiding my hometown values and the predominant religion by riding my horse, Christopher.

Even as a child, after my accident, I *saw* people with new eyes. When I went to the predominant church with friends, I remember thinking, What is all this pomp and ceremony? Why is everyone acting so false and strange? I just *knew* something phony was going on. I now realize those people were and are disillusioned and confused.

On my eighth birthday, I was baptized into the church. According to Mormon beliefs, children are baptized at eight-years-old to remove all theirs sins and begin a new future. At the age of eight, what sins could I have possibly racked up?

Was it the little white lies? My budding skepticism? The ice cream that mysteriously disappeared from the freezer? I was told if I weren't baptized would I not be allow in heaven. My conclusion then is the same as it is now: You get baptized because it is the first step in the churches efforts to control you for the rest of your life. It starts you thinking about sin and about being a sinner. If they can convince you that you are a bad person, they control you. I wonder if all churches are like the Mormons? Does anyone who believes in organized religion really think for themselves?

Even as a child, I saw the disillusionment on the faces of the people at church. When I asked questions about the book of Mormon, no one had answers. In fact, I had the feeling that my questions were viewed as evil. I had questions with no answers; I still do.

The women at the church talked mostly about the men. Men were this, men were that. Men were the sources of strength and knowledge. Women were taught to obey and be lesser of the two genders. Men were the bosses and women did the work. I tired quickly of lessons that I never understood and failed to agree with. Ultimately, I shut the *guidance* from the church off and I left this stifling environment.

I soon went off on my own, spending a lot of time alone in nature. I spent many days of my childhood atop my horse Christopher, lazily exploring the foothills of the mountains surrounding my hometown. I ventured off and lost any sense of time passing. Chris and I meandered from one place to another. I sat atop this beautiful steed and mused; fantasizing about who I might be when I grew up and wondering what the future might have in store for me. I breathed in nature and exhaled peace. I found solitude in nature's nurturing. Contemplation and nature were one and the same. If there is a God he or she can be found in the quiet gracefulness of nature.

While I say I was alone, I wasn't really alone. Christopher, the magnificent, was my companion. I was only a small girl and he was a beautiful giant horse, I was never fearful of him. He was my best friend and confidant. We wandered around the fields behind the house for endless hours. I didn't need a saddle or reins. I would lay on his back and he would just take me wherever he wanted to go. I was happy to be along for the ride. I lounged this way then that way, gazing up at the treetops or clouds. I made up songs of wild adventures and he listened contently. He loved to eat sunflowers and we would graze from one group to the next.

I could pull Chris by the nose and he followed like a little puppy. The neighborhood kids crowded around or even walked right underneath him and he wouldn't move. He was my gentle giant. All I had to do was wander out into the backyard and call his name and he came running. Sometimes, Chris and I ventured far out into the foothills and didn't make it home until long after dark. I was never afraid; I knew he would return me safe and sound. My mom hated it. She still worried because of my accident, it left her uneasy and frightened for years. I realize now my mother was worried about something else as well; I was a girl and although it was a different time and place, it was still dangerous for girls out alone at night. I couldn't have had a better friend or companion than Christopher. He was my ticket to the world of peace and nature. What better way could I have had to find the seclusion I needed to escape the false reality that was trying to control me.

Not counting my sweet Viking father, Christopher proved to be the only male I have completely trusted to this day.

If I could only live my life without a care in the world like I once did sitting on the back of sweet Christopher I could be at peace. Too bad we can't go back to those sweet trouble free days of childhood. We must live now in the present.

Still, I know my past shapes my future. What am I going to repeat and what am I going to do differently?

Chapter Nine
Airport

It's a rainy Monday and I am at the airport again. An older Asian man walks slowly along the concourse, oblivious to the sea of humanity rushing past him. It is as if he is from another time; his hands are clasped behind his back and his gaze is set on the tile floor in front of him. He slowly looks one way then the other. Following him must be his wife, she is carrying a suitcase and making sure to stay a few feet back. When he slows, she does as well. They appear to be from a culture where the man is still the leader and the woman the follower. I wonder if *our* relationships would last longer or be more fulfilling if we were like them?

Next, I see a brassy-looking woman dressed to the nines and ordering her three children and husband around. She has a nasty look on her face and they appear intimidated, like obedient dogs following wherever she orders them to go. She points to a spot next to the wall and tells them to go stand there. She gives them the once over, eyeballing them up and down, making sure they are presentable then checks the Blackberry she carries in her left hand. She is the leader and the one making the decisions. Her husband is well dressed and handsome but carries his defeat in his posture, his shoulders curve forward and down.

I feel lucky to have found Arthur. So far, he hasn't criticized me or told me once what to wear. He doesn't want to change a thing about me - or if he does, he hasn't uttered a word of it. He is certainly not a Harvey-Milk-Toast kind of man. If he has something to say, he says it - forcefully if necessary. When Jonny was talking back to me recently, he stepped forward and said, "Stop talking to your mother that way. Quit being a jerk! She is your mother, give her the respect she deserves!" Jonny was shocked, and for an instant I thought he was going to say something smart-assed, but decided against it.

Arthur treats our relationship as if we are equals. I have never had a man like him. I smile just thinking about him. I am truly in love with this one. He would never consider making a decision that impacts both of us without talking to me first. He doesn't assume that my money is his; and, he is a hard worker who has a real drive for success.

Now, two very gay men have stopped and are embracing in front of the brassy woman and her family. The gay men are all over each other. It is a separation scene, one is leaving and the other staying. Will they be true to each other, gays are notorious cheaters. The family against the wall are watching intently, looking but trying not to be noticed looking. Why are gay people so fascinating to straights?

I attract gay men everywhere I go. They see me in a crowd and want to touch, smell, feel and get close to me. I love it. I can be me without the concern of being too friendly or saying something innocent and having them misunderstand. Straight men just want to sleep with me; perhaps they are interested in a friendship or even a relationship but the first instinct is sex. I should be complimented and I am - especially knowing how many other women would love to have some (any) attention. But, it is such a turn-off to have straight men lying, deceiving and acting like fools to get into me into bed.

It would be so fun and wonderful to have straight men hanging around and not wanting to sleep with me. On the other hand, it may not be all that good. The tension between men and women is already intense and I'm really not friends with most of my past boyfriends. When I'm finally finished with them, I really don't want to have them around any more.

Straight men want you until they have you - then it all changes. They become indifferent and forget to come home or forget whose bed they are jumping into. It is all about the chase. Once they have you, it's on to the next challenge. It's best to keep them at a distance, to stay mysterious and unattainable. That way, they keep sniffing around and wanting you. I think men are constantly thinking they could be with this one or that one - is it an inborn, uncontrollable thought process? One of those biological survival of the fittest things? Some process deep within that says: impregnate as many women as possible so your genes will continue into the next generation? Or, some insatiable horniness caused by hormones? Women certainly know about the power of hormones.

Personally, I love to be admired and wanted from afar. I know an older man who is handsome and a successful book author. He is the college professor type, sophisticated and worldly, and treats me with respect - we are equals. He told me once that all an older man wants from a younger woman is for her to touch the edge of his cowboy hat. When I asked him to explain, he said, 'Older men will admire your youth and beauty but don't need to own or possess you like younger men. We just want you to acknowledge that we are still alive by touching the edge of our cowboy hat.' When men look at me with that certain look but do not approach or hit on me, I like it. It makes me feel truly attractive and desirable - not just a piece of meat for their consumption.

The rain is coming down in sheets now. I can't see the mountains at the horizon or even the planes out on the tarmac. I feel my optimism slipping away and the negative internal dialogue beginning again. Is this life I have created truly meaningful and worthy?

To each thing there is a season, or so the song goes. I think it is true though, if we listen to ourselves we know when it is time to change our lives. I feel some deep undercurrent at work inside me, pushing and prodding me to change my life in some significant and even profound way. This era is over and I need to move on - some place where life is happening and excitement rules the day.

The fear of making the wrong decision plagues me. I want the unknown; to go away with Arthur, to cut and run from this enterprise I have created, but what if it is a mistake? If I give up my established business and clients and runaway and it doesn't work, I am totally screwed. On the other hand, I started with nothing and I suspect I can start over again. It might be fun to remake myself.

I am always afraid of what the outcome might be, so I sit and wait - and do nothing. I realize it doesn't matter what I do. It is what it is. I should have left long ago. It was a wrong decision to be a business owner in this city. I feel as if I am wasting my time - my life. My Chi has left. Will I get it back? I sometimes make decisions because I am willful and unwilling or unable to admit I'm wrong. I sometimes feel it is impossible to change the path I'm on.

I can't let anyone know I'm weak and feel I *must* persevere at all costs. But who or what am I going to persevere for? For Jonny, who only wants to see me happy? For a man who will leave me as soon as I get my emotions involved? I've made so many mistakes and don't want to make any more. On the other hand, I do believe the universe only gives us what we can handle. When we are on the wrong path we lose our hum. The truth is, I've never felt a hum as a business owner. Business is about commerce and for many of us it never keeps its hum for very long. It turns very quickly into all work and no play.

I remember September 11, 2001, I was driving down the road and thought how lucky all those people were to have gone to the other side. They had gone home. I believe there are no accidents. For them, the hardship and struggle was over. For everyone left behind, for each of us, we have to continue to continue. It is all very tiring and all our business goals seem unworthy in the light of our final destination. We can't take any of our material wealth or accomplishments with us. We should spend our days doing what fulfills our heart and souls most - making sure our life vibrates with a sweet hum. Sometimes, I get really depressed and feel that I am holding on by a thread. I seem to loss all emotional attachment for everything, being a mother, a business owner, having nice things - little truly matters.

Is life a seemingly endless series of days where we accomplish nothing of true importance? Do we just follow our temporal desires and the demands of economics throughout our lives until we die and it has all been for some entirely wasted or futile existence?

When I saw the world separate before me - that wintry day as a child sleigh riding - I knew it wasn't my time and I was here for a reason, something important and worthwhile. I have had glimpses of this meaningful future but as yet I haven't arrived there. When we have a near death experience, all the superfluous things we strive for fall by the wayside and we glimpse what is really important. I have spent most of my life pursuing that illusive vision of true meaning and asking myself, why?

In the moments after my accident, I remember slipping further and further away from this world and it was good. When I started moving back towards life again I didn't want to go. Please don't make me go back, I remember saying to myself. Sometimes, I think the reality of it is, I am still mad about coming back. I would rather be there - wherever that is - than here.

Was my reason for living to be a mother? A struggling yet always hopeful business owner? A person who has no idea what her calling or true purpose on this plain really is? Where do we go to get all the pieces that fit together to form the puzzle that tells us the answer? Is my goal to influence people to seek their greatness in hopes they will become great? Or, do we let them suck the Chi out of us, leaving us empty and struggling until we can get back on our feet? I have helped many people thinking my good deeds would return to me. If it is true, why do I continue to struggle and when will someone return the favor? When is enough, enough? What happens to us when we wake up one morning and realize that we don't want to do this any more? Who will help us find our way to our true destiny?

I hear the announcement for my flight. I see my reflection in the rain soaked window. I like what I see but perhaps its because I work in the beauty business. Appearances are never the whole truth.

Chapter Ten
Arthur

A few months after moving in, Arthur lays it on me.

"I really want to move! I need to get out of here."

"You what?" I blurt out, dumbfounded.

"I can't stand this place - all the religious fanatics and hypocrites. I just hate it."

Oh boy, this sounds familiar. Mister New York all over again! He never planned on liking me; I was a mistake. He wanted to move away before we even met. He just conveniently failed to inform me. He wanted to have me around to play with until he left. Why is it the men I choose always want to get away from here? I can't stop myself from thinking it's me. Is it really about me? Do they really want to get away from me?

"What about me - and us?"

"We'll see . . . " he says, his voice trailing off.

We'll see! Oh boy. That sounds promising. I've tried the long distance thing and I don't want to do it again. I didn't say a word to Arthur. I wasn't going to start nagging or trying to be his mother either. If he wants to leave, I can't stop him. Why couldn't he just include me in the move? I have no problem with change. I would like to get out of this insipid community just as much as he would.

Am I doing something wrong? Am I putting out some kind of energy that is telling the men I really like to leave - pronto? How can a person spend every waking moment with someone and then one day just up and decide to leave? What is this anyway? Why do men get involved with me just long enough to leave? This madness needs to stop!

I've always hoped that some thing great will turn into some thing even greater. Does anyone else feel that way? If that isn't going to happen, let it end quickly so I can grab the ground again before it slaps me back down onto it. I really care about Arthur. I see how when he is stressed he grabs his paint leg and smoothes the wrinkle out with his hand. If he is really heated, he paces the room. I know when the allergies from the dog or the environment are going to get him. I know when at night something is stressing him out by the way he snores. I know the look in his eyes when he wants to know more but isn't sure how to go about asking.

After a long day at the salon, I retire to my regular hang out. The place has my favorite champagne by the glass.

Arthur calls, "Where are you?"

"Rivers. Care to join me?"

"I'm on my way."

Arthur is the most charismatic man I have ever known. As he enters the restaurant, he has a huge smile on his face and jokes with the staff and everyone he meets. He is wearing a white short sleeve shirt and black paints. On his head, has a beautiful black beret, something a painter in Paris might wear.

He leans over and kisses me. It is something I long for, it is just a peck, but if he doesn't do it I find myself missing it and wondering if something is wrong.

"Where did you get the hat? It reminds me of the cartoon character, Pepe le Pew."

He smiles and we kiss again. I can't take my eyes off him. I'm his . . . in a way I'm really not wanting what was happening to happen. Does that make sense? I'm in love.

The phone rings. "Hi Mom."

It's his mother. They talk for a few minutes, his dad is on the other phone. Arthur's parents live in Phoenix.

"She's right here," he tells her. "Do you want to talk to her?"

He hands me the phone and I talk to his parents

for a few minutes.

"I've heard a lot about you," his mother tells me. "I can't wait to meet you."

"I've heard a lot about you, too. When are you coming up?"

She is going to ride a bus up to help Arthur with a business predicament. They seem like delightful people. I hand the phone back to him.

Before Arthur arrived, I already had a glass of champagne, now I'm finishing my second.

After he hang ups, I ask, "What have you told your parents about me?" I am curious and nervous.

"That I have met this really fun chick that I think they should meet."

"Oh, really?"

The waiter arrives and we order dinner and the subject of what he tells his parents about me is tabled.

When the dinner tab arrived, he eyes it and nearly falls off his chair. Champagne by the glass - my brand anyway - is pricey.

I laugh, "I'll get the champagne."

His expression is funny and priceless. It looks as if he forgot his wallet and doesn't know what to do.

He takes a big gulp of air and swallows. He assures me it is no problem. "Anything for you, babe."

Chapter Eleven
Cabin Man

As time passes we tend to put up walls and keep behind them. Not just for ourselves but for our children. It's not so easy for children to understand why people come and go in our life. I can only hope my son, Jonny, realizes why people come and go. Some people just have a bad influence on us and we need to leave them behind so we can be healthy and move forward. Somewhere along the line, I decided to make a promise that I wouldn't let anyone around my son. I knew that the men I would be involved with would not be there for the long haul.

I have an appointment with my astrologer, I call her my therapist. After some calculations she says, "Tonya, it is time for you to get out there and start dating again."

"Really?" I responded, smiling.

"I can see that you are about to meet a wonderful man . . . maybe more than one."

"After all the losers?"

"Forget them. One must endure the losers first. The real men come later."

"More than one, huh?"

"Yes. But only one of them will be Mr. Fabulous."

"Well, okay. If you say so."

"Darling Tonya, don't be so pessimistic."

"I'm trying not to be, but I can't tell you how many . . . "

"Enough of the past!" she interrupts. "Worrying does not empty tomorrow of its trouble, it empties today of its strength."

"Oh . . ."

The next day a girl at the salon tells me about a man. She thinks we would be perfect for each other and wants to line us up for a blind date. I had been hiding behind work for months, and since my therapist told me to get out there, I decided to go for it.

She gave me all the details, height, weight, hair color (very important) and about his current status. Single. Divorced. No kids. He called a day or two later and invited me to a comedy club for dinner and a show.

Taylor was a gentleman and treated me with respect and consideration. After the third date, I realized I hadn't been able to get a word in edgewise. The first night, he talked through every comedian's act and went on and on about himself and the difficult day he had to endure. The next two dates were just as bad, nonstop Taylor this and Taylor that . . .

I was forced to endure ten hours of nonstop talk about . . . Taylor. Apparently, he had no interest in me, my life, my views or those of anyone else. At first, I took it personally but soon realized it wasn't about me, it was about him. He just couldn't get enough of himself. I imagined him standing in front of a mirror looking at himself when he called me. When he called the salon, I often put the phone on the counter and went about my work. Occasionally, I would pipe-up, 'Yeah, uh huh,' or "yeah, oh really." It was cruel but everyone at the salon thought it was hilarious. One of Taylor's most treasured subjects was the question, why do all my relationships end? Why do women dump me?

Well, Taylor my friend, far be it my duty to inform you that you might want to shut the fuck up once in a while. Unfortunately, Taylor needed someone who would sit in a corner quietly and be pretty, something I am not able to do. I have opinions.

Next was Kent, the cabin man. From the very moment I saw him, I thought, I'm going to spend the rest of my life with this man. Have you ever had the feeling when you meet someone they will be in your life for a very long time?

After playing phone tag for about a month, Kent showed up at the salon unannounced. I had just left for lunch. What are the odds? I never leave during the day but I decided to head out on the day he showed up. I couldn't believe it.

I asked Tina, the front desk girl, what he was like.

"Tan, stalky and had a nice build," she told me. "He had a voice that would make you melt. He had blonde hair and blue eyes."

"What else?"

"What more do you want? I don't know. He was older." Tina is nineteen-years-old and anyone older than twenty-five is a geezer.

My imagination ran wild. I was half heartedly happy I had left. I couldn't believe that he had shown up. I was ecstatic.

We finally met at Royces, a poplar private club. I was early, it was Wednesday the night before Thanksgiving. I sat in a corner and drank wine - to calm my nerves.

In walks this gentleman who reminded me of a surf bum. He was wearing shorts and a tee shirt. He had a nice build, was tan and had short blonde messy hair. He motions to me and walks over and gives me a big hug, as if we knew one another. We launched into a deep and fun talk about our lives. We were like old friends having a great time. We discussed everything, where we grew up, what we do for fun, our past relationships, family history.

Kent had been married before. "We met in college," he told me, "fell in love and married after I graduated. We were young and I think that was our biggest mistake. We took the relationship as far as we could then couldn't come up with a next step . . . so we decided the next step should be marriage."

He became a workaholic and within a few years he and his wife led separate lives.

Looking into my eyes he told me, "One day I came home early and found her in bed . . . with another woman!"

I was shocked, "Oh Kent, I'm so sorry."

"It would have been bad enough had it been a man, but can you imagine finding your spouse with someone of the same sex?"

"What did you do?"

"Stripped down and jumped in with them."

Kent had a mercurial glint in his ice blue eyes. I was speechless, trying to get an image of the scene in my head. At first, I thought he might be playing a not-so-funny joke on me.

"Oh," I answered, not really sure of what I

thought.

"Yeah, two weeks later, it got worse." He gave me a sideways glance. "I pulled into the drive way and saw my bosses car . . . "

"No!" I blurted out.

"Yep. Found my boss - who happened to be my best friend - and my wife in bed having sex."

I was afraid to ask what happened next.

At closing time, he asked me, "Would you like to come over to my place for an after dinner drink."

"Sure," I answered and followed him up a nearby canyon in the Wasatch Mountains to a quant cabin in an exclusive area. It was magical. The night was dark and liquid and I was swimming in excitement, lust and passion.

Over the next few months we dated on a regular basis. Kent was the most romantic man I ever met. I think it came naturally, just a part of his character. It was the way he held my hand, the way he made certain my wine glass was filled, the way he touched me . . . the way he . . .

We spend many lovely intimate nights at his cabin. He was an excellent cook and prepared wonderful meals. We sat on the couch, watched the fire burn and talked about life. Kent could talk about any subject with ease, unlike me who was still having difficulty discussing my past and how my life evolved as it had. I had never been with an older man before and chalked some of this ability to be himself up to his age. He never actually told me how old he was; I knew it was a sensitive issue so I just didn't go there. The truth is, I didn't care.

Most of our time together was spent at his cabin, and after a while I began to suspect I was his hidden pleasure. Someone he wanted for sex and companionship but not someone to be with in public.

One day at work, while discussing the blind dates I had been having, my client told me about a man she thought I might like. She said he was dating someone else right now but he would probably like to meet me.

Guess who? Kent.

"That is just great!" I told her. "I have been dating him, too."

She told me her friend's name, Leslie, and said they had been seeing each other for months. She invited me to a party where Leslie was expected to attend. In the interim, my client told Leslie - the other woman - or am I the other woman - about me.

At the party, Leslie started asking me questions, quizzing me about how long we had been seeing each other and wanting to know the current status of our relationship. She was older but attractive and apparently had just passed through the throes of an ugly divorce. Kent was the first man she had dated. She seemed nervous and on edge; I certainly was not going to get into a fight over whether he wanted to be with me or her. She probed with questions that were really none of her business. She asked, 'Have you been intimate with him?' I refused to answer and just stood there laughing. To me, it was funny. I don't know if she thought I was funny, nor did I care.

Later that evening, I headed over to Kent's house. He was surprised to see me but was his usual, romantic self.

"I just left a party," I started, "and it turned out to be a very interesting and informative evening."

"Oh really," he said, taking the bait, "What was so interesting and informative?"

"Yeah, well . . . okay." I started, "I met the other woman you've been seeing. Leslie. You know. . . "

The color drained from his face. His eye dropped and he knew he was busted. Mister conversationalist, who could talk about anything to anyone, anywhere and anytime, was speechless.

"Yeah, I don't think she's very happy right now. She likes you a lot."

After a moment of silence, he said, "I think you

should go home. I need to be alone."

"So, that's all you have to say?"

"I'll call you." His tone sounded as if I were to fault for exposing his duplicity.

My question is, why is it that when we sleep with someone the majority of us immediately think the whole world has stopped spinning and now we are exclusive to that one person? We somehow instantaneously conclude that we are in a committed relationship or are on track to be married soon. Personally, I've never felt that way. I was just going with the flow.

After work the next day, I found Kent had left a message on my machine. He didn't want to see me anymore. Leslie and my client showed up at his place after I left and had given him the third degree. Poor boy.

Was this my fault? If you are going to see more than one person, you need to let the other(s) know. I was seeing more than one person and Kent knew it. Why couldn't he have been just as upfront and honest. Now, he blames me for his dishonesty. I just laughed it off and went about my business.

Two weeks later, Kent called. He apologized for the mean message left on my machine. I said, "I didn't see anything so wrong. I didn't know why you were so mad at me. What had I done? I knew we weren't exclusive. We had just started dating. I was seeing other people, too."

He told me about how the two women showed up at his place and let him have it. What a way to win a man over - bring your friend to help ream him out. I told him I was not angry. We were just dating - nothing more, nothing less.

I saw him regularly at the cabin. I will always be the secret girlfriend. I am okay with it. After all, I wasn't about to let him into my life with Jonny.

I wanted Jonny to have normal relationships with women. What is normal, anyway? The fear of commitment, rebounds, one night stands, wondering about or desiring other people? Who was I to say?

I continued to see Kent on and off, it has now lasted many years. He truly listens to me and he has inspired me in business. Maybe that is what he is all about. He has never met my son.

Deep inside, Kent loves me. When he is lonely he calls. He moved away a few years ago but around the holidays I am sure to get a phone call from him. He always wants me to drop everything and run right over into his arms. I have done this in the past but it is not part of my present and will not be part of my future.

Chapter Twelve
Airport

Standing in the middle of the concourse, hundreds of people pass by in a minute. They are every size and shape and color and nationality. The only thing they have in common is they are in a hurry, and are part of the human race. Something about western society seems to wring out the calmness in people and replace it with the frantic notion of needing to get somewhere fast.

When we are home, going about our lives at a slower pace, we dream of stepping into the world of transience, of being on our way to somewhere romantic or filled with adventure, somewhere that life is happening - somewhere other than where we are. We want to be alive while we are alive.

Who are these people? What awaits them at the end of today's flight. I see an older couple clinging to one another as the stream of humanity breaks against them like the vortex of a swirling eddy in a river, flowing around and past them. I hope when I get their age, I have a companion who can help me find my way through the maze of life's concourses. Just as the older couple is lost in the crowd, I see what I think are probably newlyweds on their way to some honeymoon resort. They are beautiful and filled with love and passion, I can see it in their eyes. The beginning of love, the first year or two, is a treasured thing.

Here comes a group of Asian men who meet a group of Persian-looking men - handsome, dark and swarthy. After a brief conversation they move off somewhere, disappearing around a corner. They are dressed in the universal uniform of business: a dark suit, white shirt and tie. I like standing at the center of this mass of humanity, coming and going, fearful and self assured, young and old, happy and heartbroken. I feel a part of something much larger than myself here, like I'm a bee in a hive, doing my part but unaware of the grand over-arching purpose. Do we *really* have a purpose or is this fury just sound and movement that amounts to nothing?

I'm on my way back to my subservient city. I can see the airplane out the window, it is brand new. Stepping inside the pilot announces that the plane *is* brand-new, this flight is only its fourth flight. The air conditioner doesn't work, and they are working the kinks out. Lucky us. A girl two rows up is shouting into her cell phone as if unaware she is surrounded by other passengers.

"Oh my God. Really?"

"She just got engaged."

"I'm on my way back right now."

"How big is it?"

I hope she is talking about the ring.

"Platinum or Gold?"

"Oh good, he has my approval."

"How did he propose?"

"Was it romantic?"

"Oh my god, how romantic!"

From what I gather, he had taken her up to the lake where they go quite often. He proposed on a moonlit canoe ride in the middle of the lake. How lovely.

I have been seeing Arthur exclusively for two years now. We have been living together for six months. No ring or moonlit canoe ride yet. He is picking me up at the airport. When I say exclusively, I mean no more Cabin Man, no more New York man, and no more no mores.

Arthur is going to see a psychic tonight. He saw her one other time and she seemed to know things about him. What I didn't know was that the first time she told him he would soon be leaving for parts unknown, and he was not coming back. Arthur hates Mormon Utah and wants to die somewhere else. He told me, 'I don't want to be caught dead in Utah.' His desire to be gone started long before we began dating. For me, it is all too familiar. Mr. New York had to get away, too. He hated this place; and, same goes for Mr. Cabin Man. Without a word, he sold his properties and relocated. Why is it they love you and then leave?

I feel like a flight attendant. I lead them to the concourse of their destiny and then they are gone. Am I about to do it again? I've never minded helping people get on their way, no matter what it meant to me personally. I have been secretly hoping someone would be around to help me get going on whatever my true destiny is suppose to be. Karma.

Later, after his appointment with the psychic, I expect to get a call from Arthur at work. Normally, he would have called me to tell me what happened but I didn't hear from him. He has been home over an hour - something is not right. I dial his number.

"So, what did she have to say?"

"You'll just have to come home and listen."

As I drive home, I realize that since we have been together I've really had a great time. We don't fight or argue, there is no drama; our level of communication is deep, and we have the best sex I've ever had. The great sex is either him or maybe because I'm in my thirties now. I am concerned though tonight,

I could tell there was something peculiar about his voice and his not calling after his appointment.

He greets me at the front door and encloses me in his arms, holding me tight and keeping me close.

"Want to have sex before . . . or after you listen to the tape?"

"I don't know," I say, suddenly frightened. "Should we have sex before I listen?"

"It might be fun," he says in his nervous, laughing voice. Now, I know something is wrong.

"Lets listen first," I say putting my purse on the counter and sitting on the living room couch.

Arthur starts the tape and sits next to me.

She tells him he doesn't belong here. She sees him living somewhere in the south.

Okay, I can see that. He doesn't like our behave state any more than I do.

She tell him he's going to go into real estate or property management of some sort.

I can see that. He has wanted to sell the salon for a long time. He says he wants out and that he's never looking back. Then it happens, the freak out!

"This is your love life?" she starts turning cards.

"It is really wonderful, great!" Arthur pipes in.

"I can tell it is the best its ever been, but it's only going to get better."

Okay, I can see that.

She continues, "But not with your current partner . . . you are going to meet a natural blonde with blue eyes."

"So, she's (ME!) not going away with me."

"No, she is karma. You know karma can last an hour, a day, a year, etc."

"Yeah, really? I know." Arthur says surprised. "Are we going to be friends?"

"Yes."

Okay. At this point, I am holding back tears. I sit there listening to the rest of the tape, and fighting to withhold my emotions.

How could this psychic say his "love life's the best its ever been but it's only going to get better - with someone else?" Oh yeah, and the, "you'll be friends," remark! Whatever I am, it's not friends with my past boyfriends and lovers - of course, there are a few exceptions.

After the tape Arthur is all over me, ready for some action in the bedroom. The sex is good but I feel nothing; I fight back tears.

Later, his cell phone rings and I dress as he answers it. We are scheduled to go to a Feng Shui workshop but while he is on phone, I decide I need to be alone and go for a drive. I needed to digest what I had just heard. How can you be with someone and never have any issues and then a psychic tells you the relationship is over? As I leave I tell him I will be back later. He seems confused. I have never just left before.

I drove aimlessly - sobbing and ranting - until I remember a stylist at the salon asked me to give her a ride to the workshop. Once at the salon, everyone crowds around. They can see I have been crying and want to know what happened. I can't think straight so I say nothing.

Arthur calls just as we arrive at the workshop. I don't want to answer so I let it ring. A few minutes later, he tries again.

"Hello."

"What are you doing?"

"I just want to be alone."

"I thought we were going to this class?"

"I need to be alone."

"Okay," he says.

The next week at the salon I spent a lot of time either in my office crying or pretending every thing was all right. My eyes were red and swollen but I tried to act happy. Pretending is something I don't have much talent for, so the entire salon was in an uproar trying to figure out what was happening. Everyone - employees, clients, vendors - asked, 'What's wrong?' or 'Why are you crying?' I was a zombie and didn't answer. I really needed some help, fast.

My therapist is the most fabulous, ultimate queen of therapy, and if anyone can help me, she can. My whole world has been shaken up by the psychic I now call, "The Devil."

Not that I need all the answers, but the idea that I am nothing more than Karma and soon to be replaced by a natural blonde needed to be addressed.

My therapist knew something was terribly wrong and rushed to me, giving me a big hug. Her mere presence has a calming effect and I sat down and tried to be at peace.

Five months earlier, I had seen her about a big financial decision I was about to make. I've always felt I made the wrong choices about money and business and was tired of it. The fear of making another mistake made me ask for another opinion. It isn't that I don't trust myself, it's that I don't listen to myself. For some reason, I need affirmation from an outside source. At what point in my life will I actually think for myself? She told me the universe had called my name and that I wasn't even looking for it. What does this mean? She answered, 'It is in your chart. Only you can decipher it.'

She asked, "What happened a week ago on the fourteenth?"

What! How does she know the date? She just gave me the date of Arthur's psychic reading! I am shocked and in awe. How could that have shown up on an astrology chart?

I told her about the psychic and the tape.

"You are depressed," she started. "I want you to hang in there. This is all going to end on March nineteenth, but you need to say how you feel. I know you get all choked up when it comes to expressing your feelings but you need to get it out."

"Okay," I answer, taking what she said to heart. I can do it! It took a few weeks to get up the nerve and to decide what I was or wasn't going to say to Arthur.

I was haunted by the similarity of how life plays out. I had already had two men leave me for blondes and two others leave town after I fell in love with them. I kept telling myself, this is similar but it is not the same. It happened in my past and I don't want it happening in my future. This is similar, but not the same. While it might appear to be similar, the ending would be different.

Chapter Thirteen
Men - Not Everything Washes Off

Some men I've known think all a woman needs is a man to take care of her. This idea must have come from a different time and place. Who knows when or where this idea took root but today, the opposite is the rule. It goes like this: the woman continues to work, she is the primary provider, she pay all the bills, they live in her house, she puts up with the man's ex-wife and kids, often paying his child support, she cooks and cleans, and she is expected to be sexy too - and put out on demand. The man's job is to take the woman to dinner or a movie or skiing or snowmobiling occasionally. If something breaks, he tries to fix it. Oh, I forgot, the man tries to tell the woman what to wear, where to buy it and how much to pay.

It was New Year's Eve and I didn't have a date. A client, Lana, asked, "What are you doing for New Year's Eve."

"Nothing."

"Dale has a friend I would like to set you up with. Want to join us?"

"Sure, why not."

Dale and Lana have been together for about

six months. Apparently, he hasn't been very nice to her. Something of a sly guy; you know, one of those you have to watch. Like some men, he thinks he's in demand, handsome, intelligent and unique. According to her, if she goes to the rest room when they are out, Dale is across the room introducing himself to another woman when she returns. He is an airline pilot and feels this gives him some extra allure or cache, as if he were a world famous heart surgeon or Hollywood leading man. His job take him out of town often and Lana is suspicious he has other women.

The celebration is at a friend of Lana's house in a nice neighborhood. As soon as I arrive I meet Bobby - he too is an airline pilot. He is tall, dark, has piercing green eyes and curly dark hair. He is also twenty year my senior. A man's age has never been that important to me, in fact at that time, I really didn't care. Bobby is in great shape and brags about going to the gym everyday.

The intimate dinner party includes about twenty guests, all of whom seem to know one another. Bobby takes my coat and runs to get me a glass of merlot. Sitting on the couch and he wants to know all about me. Hmm, this might turn into something. From the beginning, we are quite comfortable with each other. I decided the new year was worthy of a good celebration so I let Bobby fill my wine glass again and again.

Suddenly, there's a commotion in the hallway. It's my friend, Lana, hollering at Dale.

"What are you doing talking to them when you have me?"

Apparently, Dale was doing what Dale does, talking to a group of women who gathered in the kitchen.

"Aren't I good enough for you?" she demand.

"Come on Lana, its New Year's Eve, lighten up." His response is muted and he is embarrassed. Bobby whispers that Lana is insecure and she put Dale through these inquisitions - in front of everyone - often. After their disagreement, she plops down next to me.

"I think I'm much prettier than they are. Don't you?"

"Of course," I agree. Lana is very attractive: tall, thin and fit; she works out regularly. What is it about women that makes them so insecure? She has nothing to worry about. I saw what Dale was doing - nothing.

After a few minutes, she gets up and goes down the hallway.

The next thing I know, Dale grabs his coat and storms out the door. He doesn't stop to explain or say good night to the host or any of us. Lana is right behind him. She has murder in her eyes. From the hallway, another woman exits a bedroom where Dale had just come from. Well . . . I'm glad I brought my own car.

Why have a relationship if you fight all the time? Is it the make up sex? Or the excuse to have sex? Why are so many people miserable in relationships they have spent so much time and energy trying to make it work? I would much rather be alone than to be with someone who was unacceptable or who is unhappy with me.

I stay late and drink too much. Bobby tries to maneuver me into agreeing to come to his place but I know what this means so I decline; besides, I have an angel at home that I need to be with. Bobby asks for my number and I go home.

The next day Lana calls and tells me I was a big hit at the party. Bobby was quite smitten. He wants to see you again, she says. She apologized for her behavior and blamed Dale for being a stinker. I told her I'd given Bobby my number and would wait to hear from him.

The next night I go out alone to a local bar. I frequent the place because it is close to work and I enjoy listening to the band. Usually, some of the girls from the salon show up and we have a good time talking and just hanging out.

I notice a guy at the bar who looks familiar. He is giving me *that* look and I knew sooner or later he would stop by our table. He was handsome and rugged-looking - a man's man. When he finally consumes enough liquid courage, he makes his way over. After introducing himself, I realize I knew him, he worked for my father years ago. I was in high school and he paid a good deal of attention to me. I guess he had a thing for me; it was the red hair. His father once made a comment about red heads being hellfire and great in bed, and he wanted to find out for himself.

"I've always admired your folks," he says, after a few more beers, "they seem to have such a great marriage. I could tell they like each other, your dad was always kidding your mom . . . and they raised all you good looking girls. I just wish I could find someone and have that kind of marriage."

I wasn't about to enlighten Rick on my parent's sometimes difficult and tenuous marriage so I just smiled and went along with it.

"Thanks," I said. "Yeah, I love them. I'll tell them what you said."

"Yeah," he went on, "That's what I want, a good marriage with kids, like your parents . . . I'll bet you are just like your mother. You'll make a great wife and a mother to a whole bunch of good looking, smart kids."

I had had enough fairy tale marriage talk. "No thanks," I say in a deadpan voice, "not for me, thank you. I'm not anything like my mother."

"You can't be serious!" He shouted, the beer now talking for him. "Just look at you. You will make some man a great wife - like your mother - and have a whole slew of kids."

Some advice for men: If a woman tells you she is not interested in marriage or children, believe her.

Before I left, Rick asked if I wanted to go out sometime and I told him sure. We got together for dinner and a movie a few times; it was always on my schedule and by my rules. I was still on the free food and movie routine. He kept up the sales job on marriage and kids and after a while I just tuned him out - even once pointing out a Mormon brood mare with eight or nine kids in toe. Perhaps she is available, I said, nodding in her direction.

One night he picked me up for dinner and was upset.

"What's wrong?" I asked.

"Out of the blue, I got a letter from the office of recovery services," he started. "They wanted me to take a blood test because a girl I had seen only once is saying I'm the father of her baby!"

"Are you?"

"Yup." He said, dejected. "They did a DNA test and sure enough, it was a match."

"Boy, that's something. Instant daddy. What are you going . . . "

"I don't even remember her," he interrupted. "Sheesh, it was more than six years ago. Now, I have a six-year-old son and she wants me to support him."

"I guess it only takes once." I said solemnly.

"You got that right."

He heard from friends of hers that the night they met she was out looking for a good looking guy to father her child. She is a so-called feminist and did not want to be married or have a man in her life but wanted a baby. Now, she has found out how difficult it is to be a single mother and wants help. I tell people about the power of the penis and Rick's situation is exactly what I'm talking about. No matter its size or how it is wielded, a penis can change the life of any woman who comes into contact with it.

The truth is, I don't have much sympathy for Rick. As he tells me all the particulars I have to bite my tongue and turn away so I don't grimace or worse - laugh. I mean, what was he thinking? What about a condom? Some men are just so horny they don't think about the consequences. Consequences are a woman's responsibility. Don't get me wrong, I have no sympathy for the woman either. What was she thinking? Bringing a child into a world where it is difficult enough with two parents - and she's going to do it alone. Marching to a different drummer - uh huh.

A few nights later, I invite Rick to my house for dinner. I normally don't do this and I really shouldn't have. I guess I felt sorry for him and was thinking about - pity fuck number three. I should have my head examined.

Rick, the wanna-be father is telling my son what to do within an hour of arriving. Jonny is not going for it. What have I got myself into?

Why is it we can see into other people's lives so easily, picking out the mistakes and missteps and misconceptions with clarity and knowing all the solutions to their problems, but at the same time we can't see our own mistakes and stupidity when it hits us directly in the face?

And what's wrong with me? I feel pity fuck number three coming on.

The thing is, I'm not really even interested

in him. After Jonny was safe and asleep, he asked if he could stay. I wanted to say no but didn't, so we climbed into bed and started making out. We had seen each other for nearly six weeks and we had kissed and played around a little but nothing else.

Rick is all over me. Kissing me, fondling the twins, straddling me. I think I can get into this so I move my hand down his back and around the front to find him but . . . but . . . there was nothing there! No . . . wait a minute. . . There is something there! Oh no! It can't be!"

Without thinking, I jump out of bed. "You have to leave!" I say shaking my head, "I can't do this. What is wrong with me? I am a mom for Christ's sake. This isn't right. Jonny is in the next room!"

Without a word he gets out of bed like a little pouting boy, dresses and leaves. Afterwards, I lay there stunned. He had the smallest, tiniest penis on the planet. I swear to God. I couldn't help myself and burst out into laugher. His penis was so small it was bizarre. Fully erect, it was no bigger than my pinky finger. When they say that size doesn't matter, they weren't thinking of Rick. I am sure the girl he got pregnant was surprised, too.

He called days later and I apologized and told him I had been having second thoughts. It was nothing against him but I wasn't ready for an exclusive relationship.

A few weeks passed and day or two before Valentine's Day I met a few girl friends at the geriatric ward, a club where everyone is older than our parents. After all, it's all in fun. I spot Rick across the room and I'm taken aback.

I decide to say hello and walked over just as he stood up to leave.

"Hi, Rick."

"Hello," he says coolly. "I was just leaving . . . but I'll stay for a while if you buy me a beer."

"Okay," I say, secretly feeling sorry for him because I dumped him and because of, well . . . you know. "Would you like to join us," I ask, gesturing to our table, "and meet some of my friends?"

He shakes his head from side to side, "Not really."

I can tell he is angry or hurt, probably both.

I order Rick a beer and one of my girl friends offers me a shot of tequila. We salute each other and down our shots.

"You're not buying that guy a beer, are you?" she asks.

"Just one. I feel sorry for him."

I gave Rick the beer and ask again if he would

like to join us. He declined and downed the entire beer like it was a shooter.

"As I said," he informed me, "I was just about to leave but I'll stay around if you buy me a Jack (Daniels) and a coke."

"Excuse me!" I say, now irked.

"You heard me." He said, narrowing his eyes.

"Look Rick, I supported an asshole for three fucking years, if you think I'm dumb enough to do it again you better look elsewhere."

Without a word, he steps back and threw his empty beer can at me - and missed - and then pushes past me and leaves.

Across the room, my friends are on their feet watching.

"What did you say to him?" one asks.

"Boy, he looked angry," another offered.

"He sure had a pissy look on his face." Still another sarcastically. "That was really funny, can you do it again?"

We all burst into laughter.

I couldn't help myself and told them all about Mister Pinky Finger. Everyone blushed and rocked back and forth in a fit of laughter, and we all raised our glasses in a toast to men with real penises. If you are a man with a small penis I strongly advise you to not treat a woman badly. Once the word is out, it can't be taken back.

Now, all I have to do is raise my little finger and they all know who I am talking about.

One night a few weeks later as I pulled into my driveway after work, I saw a package in the carport. It was flowers from Mr. Pinkie Finger, Rick. It was a thoughtful gesture but gift giving has become less about giving someone you like or admire a thoughtful gift and more about some other message. In this case, Rick wanted to show he was romantic and wanted to be friends again. It was more a peace offering than a bona fide or genuine gift. To bad, it wasn't going to work.

With all the so-called men in my life, I've found that the only real man I love is my son, the man of the house. I sometimes feel so badly for him. Recently, at school he was given an assignment asking, "If you had a genie what three wishes would you ask for?" He drew a Genie and placed his three wishes around it. The first wish was for all the money in the world so his mother didn't have to work so hard. The second wish was for a father; he had drawn a picture of "a dad." I immediately broke down in tears, and I never got to the last wish.

It's funny, you can give your kids pretty much

anything in the world, but you can't go buy a dad. I had asked my own Viking father to take Jonny places and spend some time with him over the years, but he was simply too busy, or would always say, "I will when he is older." How much older does he have to be, I wondered? He definitely needs some mature male energy in his life, someone he might admire and respect and perhaps model himself after, but this is one I can't offer him.

After composing myself, I called his biological father, Tom. I told him about Jonny's project and the next morning he came by before work. He seemed genuinely interested in being Jonny's father and committed to take Jonny every Monday, Wednesday and Friday. Jonny was thrilled and I think both are having a great time getting to know one another for the first time. Unfortunately, Tom who I thought was a man when we were together - so much for my judgment - is really just a big boy who has yet to grow up. This fact has an up side and a down side. Two boys in this household is one too many. We'll have to wait and see how it goes.

From the moment he arrived in our lives he started making comments and innuendos about us - he and I - and about his interest in me. No way. I suspect he thinks my call had something to do with me wanting to try again. Hurl time! The red passion that was once there is long-gone, it evaporated like the water on Mars eons ago and it is not coming back. At the same time, the other men in my life make him jealous.

One evening he arrived as Jonny and I are watching a video.

"Want to stay and hang out with us?" I ask, trying to be friendly.

"No thanks," he answered in his lanky boyish voice. "I don't need to be here and see you with one of your boyfriends."

"Whatever."

Bobby, the pilot, comes to the salon almost everyday. After our New Year's Eve date I didn't hear from him much, then he just started calling again and coming around. He just drops in after his workout as if my place of business is a hang out. He often brings something tasty and healthy for me and the staff to nibble on. He seems happy enough just to sit around, drink coffee and talk to my employees and clients. It is getting more than a bit annoying; I'm trying to work and make money.

I found out that the day after our first date, another woman he was dating arrived in town unannounced and he was occupied with her while I was dating Mr. Pinky Finger. Bobby informed me that he broke it off with the other woman in the hope he could have something with me. Okay.

As I worked on a client, she said, "I sure wish I had your figure Tonya, you are so beautiful."

"Thank you." I answered, feeling pleased. "Considering I don't have time to work out or anything, and that my diet is awful, I guess I don't look too bad."

"Yeah," Bobby pipes up, "You could afford to tone up some."

I was floored and shot him the death ray look. How dare him! Especially in front of my client.

He swallowed hard.

"You know, Bobby, if you don't like it don't look at it." I was fuming, "I can always go to the gym and get into shape, but you will always be bald."

He got my point. What right does he have to tell me I have to shape up? I wasn't about to let him see me naked ever - again. So, he wants to have something with me, aye? I don't think so.

In the midst of seeing all these men I went to see my therapist. Now, my therapist is a Tea Leaf reader.

Looking into the tea leaves, she says, "What are you doing, this isn't you."

"What do you mean?"

"Let me tell you about a girl who comes to see me." She pauses and looks over my left shoulder. "I ask this girl why she is sleeping with all these men in her life? She answers, 'This is the 90s' and every one is doing it.'

"The next time she comes in we have the same conversation. I ask again, why are you sleeping with all these men, and her answer was the same.

The next time she comes, I say, 'I can see that you have stopped sleeping with all those men.' And she answers, 'Yes, I woke up one day and realized not everything washes off.'"

I just sat there shocked and speechless.

Truthfully, I haven't been sleeping with all the men who are in my life but I am getting to the point where I realize not everything washes off.

Chapter Fourteen
Business

I am forever waiting for the hum. Some times I question if I can think for myself or make the right decisions? Do I call one of my therapists? Do I conjure up my own therapy? The truth is, my business has been less successful than I've wanted it to be. Somehow, if we become successful, we think we should start our own business. People around us, tell us to do it to. I don't know if it's a good idea. I know an artist who is a superb painter, so good she decided to open a gallery. She had to paint her tail off to pay the rent on her dream art gallery. After two years, she was exhausted and the gallery closed. Not surprisingly, everyone loved the gallery and wondered why it closed. She went back to painting and now is at peace.

The same thing is happening to me. I had success right out of the gate as a stylist; magazines and professional photographers wanted to use me for make up and hair. I had a golden touch, everything I did brought more success and money. My client list grew into the hundreds, so . . . it just seemed like a natural progression that I should open a salon. Makes sense, right? Now I work six days a week, keep a hectic pace with clients and fly from one city to the next, doing stylist exhibitions for an international hair care company. With money I make I pay for a salon that is often half filled - not for lack of customers but for lack of good dependable, talented stylists.

I spent hundreds of thousands to build and continuously upgrade my salon so its state of the art and a fabulous place to spend an hour or two. Unfortunately, no one seems to notice. I give young stylists a great opportunity in a first-class environment with enormous potential and they can't seem to get to work on time or stop complaining. I drive a Jaguar and behind my back, the stylists who rent space from me, talk about how they are paying for it - as if they are supporting me. I spend more money trying to keep my salon staffed and everyone happy than I make. Something needs to go.

Last week, I did seminars at salons in two cities. Both salons were approximately the same size and had the same number of stylists. One had her entire staff quit and go up the street to another salon. She was angry but told me it was the second time it happened. She was worried about revenue and where she could find good stylists. The other salon owner, was collecting her staff from other salons in the same general area, picking them up one by one. One was losing staff to a predatory salon down the road and the other was collecting staff who were unhappy where they were. What goes around, comes around.

One of the owners wanted to run a business and be the boss, making all the decisions and having her stylists treat her as the boss. It wasn't working. The other let her staff run the salon, giving them control over their lives, and it wasn't working either. Like my situation, they envied and blamed her for the financial success she was having. It is a no win situation. Like fashion or beauty, looks are always deceiving. If you see a perfect family, driving a Mercedes and living in a monster home, scratch the surface and you'll find out they are one step ahead of the bill collectors, a divorce is in the offing because the perfect mom and handsome dad are both having affairs and their beautiful children are bed-wetting lunatics.

I'm getting to the point where women make me want to vomit. I cut and style their hair and all I hear is complaints about husbands and kids and how unappreciated or unfulfilled they are. They don't work, they live in nice big houses, they drive expensive cars, they dress as if money is no object, they go from one vacation to the next, they have little real responsibility, but to listen to their complaints they could be Mother Teresa in a concentration camp. Sniveling and whining. Whining and crying. Crying and more sniveling. I wonder, am I getting burned-out? Am I delusional? I would just as soon slap some of them as coddle them.

Is this just a mental block from hanging on to my past? I've always made the money, struggled with the decisions, and never asked for help. What is wrong with me? Am I jealous? Perhaps. Like many girls, I was raised with the fairytale notion that some handsome, prince-like man would come and sweep me off my feet and treat me like a princess. In this fairyland, I would not have to work, or if I did, it wouldn't be too hard and I would be treated with great love and respect.

Many of the women whose hair I cut, have this kind of life and all they do is bitch. If they had to work for themselves, they would shut their mouths and appreciate what that inconsiderate and dopy husband has been doing for them all these years.

As far as men go, I seem to make one mistake after another. It has been going on for years now. Was my grandpa right? Do men want virgins? I am disgusting because I've slept with a few men and boys - or should I say wanna-be men?

I remember Thanksgiving Day when my grandfather let me know I was on the wrong track. I arrived at my parent's house for dinner and I brought my own bottle of wine. I thought it would be fun and, of course, everyone else does it. While a bottle of wine wouldn't overturn most family Thanksgiving celebrations, it was not part of my families holiday traditions. My grandfather, who had never attempted to be a part of my life, looked at me in disgust as I came through the door.

"You obviously don't know how to have a good time if you had to bring that to dinner," he commented, staring at the bottle from his perch on the living room couch.

"Good to see you, too Grandpa," I answered, wanting to put a pillow over his face and hold it for a while.

Okay, the bottle of wine wasn't about him. It was about me having a day off which I very rarely get. It was my day to relax and enjoy myself, so I just laughed that one off.

After dinner, as the women cleaned up he started the lecture.

"You know the reason you aren't married, don't you?" he asked looking at me.

"Men are afraid I'd make them go to work and not sponge off of me?" I answered, lightheartedly.

"Men want virgins and you have sinned."

"Easy for you to say, grandpa." I said picking up the potato salad and for a moment I considered tipping the bowl over his pointy bald head. "You speak for all men?" I hit back.

"When you had your son, everyone knew."

"Knew what?"

"That you were living in sin."

"Oh, no. Heavens sake!" I laugh as my mother and sisters exited the kitchen like insects escaping insecticide.

"That's why life is so hard for you," he said shaking his head. "If you would go to church and repent, it would get better for the both of you."

"No grandpa, it wouldn't. As far as the not being married, I have yet to find a man that has something to offer me that I can't offer myself. As far as my son goes, God gave me him because he knew I could handle it - unlike most men out there. And as far as the religion goes, Man created religion to evoke fear and guilt in people especially women, so they would OBEY the man. No, I don't think so. I've seen how you *men* of religion work, and I wouldn't have any of you. As far as I am concerned, God loves me as he does my son no matter what religion I do or not believe in."

Gramps scrunched up his face like he just

smelled a dog turd. Next time, I'm going to try the bowl of potato salad and see what he thinks of that.

The sorry truth is, many women listen to men like my grandfather and believe they are sinners or bad people. Every day at the salon I listen to women filled with guilt and self loathing because they committed the ultimate sin, they thought about themselves first or put themselves somewhere near the top of the list. These poor souls have the almighty fear of their husbands hanging over their heads.

Do they come to me for inspiration during the week? I suspect many are vicariously living their lives through people like me. They see independent women, making good money and want to be like us. I think they are holding out hope that some day, some way they might find out who they really are by going out on their own and living independently. Boy, do I put on a show for them. It's my stage big and bright so they want to be a part of it. They come they go, they come back again. I listen, tell them what I'd do in their place and I feel like their unpaid therapist. How many of them actually listen to me? Who knows. Crazy as it sounds, I should charge more for my services especially the therapy session.

Do women actually know how to be in-de-pen-dent? Or are they really just wishing for it? Or, is the sad truth they are consistently dependant? I find that I am not the norm. I am independent, I don't know how to act when someone truly wants to do something for me. What do they *really* want? I don't want financial security, that usually means some kind of control. Having someone control me isn't any fun, why would I want that? I didn't enjoy having my hair pulled and ripped out, the way Tom did, when I wanted to do something my way. Is it possible to be yourself and be a woman?

Women who are independent, still have the desire for a commitment. I know I do. At what point do you keep yourself without losing yourself? Take for instance Shela, a client of mine. Shela left her husband and religion at the same time. He was an alcoholic and the religion kept her pinned down and dependent. Free of both she became a wildly successful business woman. She supported her three kids better than the husband did. She met many interesting people and was transferred to wonderful locations. One day she met Mr. Fabulous who loved and accepted her for who she was. Ta, Da.

Another client was married and divorced, then had a live-in relationship as she raised her two children. When she turned fifty, the live-in left her for a younger woman and after climbing out of the pit of despair, she started dating again and found a man who was more successful, more fun and more handsome than the man who left her. She sold her house of thirty-years - not an easy thing to do because a house is security - and she and the new man build a fabulous home in the mountains. Fun, fun, fun.

Yes, ladies living in sin is very much the fabulous thing to do. It saves you some of the heartache of divorce and saves you money as well. Not that you don't have heartaches or headaches but it sure nice not paying lawyers. Just take what belongs to you and leave the rest behind.

Either I have a great relationship or I have a great business. I feel I can't have both. It has been readily apparent, it is one way or the other. Do I let it all go for a man? Or do I let him go and keep my business? There is never a clear answer at the beginning. I am swimming in my own mix of emotions and can't see a shoreline to swim too.

Being married or in a committed relationship is like being a business owner. In fact, I've been married to my business for fifteen years now. One of the biggest challenges is loyalty. I have loyalty issues. I find that I am seeking a form of loyalty. I have been loyal to relationships, business ties and personal friendships. I have spent a good deal of time and energy, buying into loyalty and maintaining it.

I have been loyal to my business but realize I'm not going to get any alimony, even after fifteen years. I feel as if my business is worth more than those around me. Arthur thinks that if its just too much of a hassle I should sell it off, piece by piece, and be done with it. Like him, I now want to get out and do something else. My client's move around; they aren't loyal. They come back when they are in a disarray, just long enough for me to get them back on track again. Then they are gone. I had been loyal in relationships only to find that you need some kind of humming, a balance of the emotional, the physical and the mental. Nothing lasts forever. Unfortunately. I've concluded there is no such thing as loyalty. It's a farce.

My all-time favorite book is, The Princess Bride. I guess it's the fairytale I dream of. That my true love will come back and do every thing "As YOU wish." Do we conjure up these illusions, and then create this in our destiny? Do our thoughts control our future? Can we change our stars? I just hope my future will be different from my past.

Arthur tells me he has never had any one love him so deeply or honestly as I do. The funny thing is, he probably never will. Will he regret the choice he is making to move away and change the future we might have together?

What do I have to offer him in the first place? His biggest night- mare is to be supporting another woman and her child. He now wants only independent women. If I leave everything I have here to go with him, I will need his financial help to reestablish myself. But I'm getting ahead of myself. He hasn't even asked me to go with him yet.

I just may be his girl for the present moment. When he leaves, he is gone. Does he secretly believe he will find the perfect blonde? I think he is still holding on to that idea. The question is, should I continue to hang in there, and even put more effort and time into it? Unfortunately, we can't buy back time.

I could go see a counselor or psychic or astrologers or palm reader and find out what they have to say. At what point do you stop getting advice and start listening to yourself? I guess the thought of the gut wrenching feeling of a break-up leaves me in a holding pattern. If he doesn't see me in his future, why do I?

Do I need to beg for a relationship? Is there really someone out there for everyone? Is it all about the vibration you put out there when you meet some one? I wasn't looking when I hooked up with him . . . I know the impact my relationships have on Jonny. He has a loss, too. Do you ever want to put that much energy into it? I see some people happy in their relationships and decisions and other sad and resentful. Some are lonely, others not. Is there a place of true bliss or is that just illusion? Is it only when death is upon us that we find these things?

Chapter Fifteen
New York Man

Making my way back home from a one day seminar, I spot a man in the airport who, at first, I was convinced was Kevin, my one time boyfriend and a big time loser. Mr. New York. The man was impeccably dressed and had an air about him, like he was a millionaire or a celebrity. As I watched him disappear down the concourse, it all came flooding back.

According to Mika, Kevin was handsome and talked as if he came from a family with resources. She didn't know why he was in Utah but he was definitely not a Utah type. He didn't have a relationship for various reasons, he'd been single too long, had trouble with his last girlfriend, he thought women were cheaters and he just hadn't met anyone who he thought was worthy.

Mika told Kevin she had someone he might be interested in: a friend who owned her own business and wasn't looking for a man to take care of her. He was interested in the details, especially about how much money I made. Kevin told Mika, 'I don't need another schemer wanting me for my money.'

I received a voice mail from Mika, apologizing

for giving Kevin my address and telling him to stop by. I just shook my head. In the afternoon, a very well groomed and well dressed man stopped at the salon and asked the receptionist for me. He seemed formal yet approachable, and while I didn't fall madly in love, he *was* a good prospect.

Later, Mika called, "Did you like him?"

"He seemed nice, but I was busy and couldn't talk."

"I think he is a millionaire!" she said, excited.

"Okay," I say, "I can handle that. How do you know?"

"He took me to his house in the avenues and it was fabulous. His mother lives there - I think she is sick and he is taking care of her. He told me the house was part of his inheritance."

A few minutes later, I take a call from him. He wants to take me to dinner. He is going to pick me up after work at the salon.

Kevin is punctual and escorts me in his luxury car to La Caille, perhaps the most expensive and ostentatious restaurant in the city. He seems equal parts of show and substance. He wants to impress me.

After three months of sporadic but enjoyable dating, I realized I knew little more about him than when we met. He is vague when asked about his family and just acts secretive, like he has something to hide. I do know one thing about him, he sees himself being famous, perhaps a celebrity. His fame will arise from music, either as a musician or record producer. I like Kevin and spending time with him, but he makes me feel as if I am on parade. I sense he wants a beautiful woman on his arm in the same way he wants to drive a showy car, wear expensive clothing, and be seen at the right clubs.

A few weeks before Christmas, while having dinner, he surprises me with his plan to leave Utah.

"Why did you want to date me," I asked, sitting up, "if you knew you were going to leave?"

"You knew I hated Utah," he said, surprised. "It can't be too much of a shock!"

"But that doesn't answer my question."

"I like you - that's why." He responded quite naturally, as if this lame explanation should suffice.

I just looked at him.

"I didn't think it would work out, that's why!"

Silence.

"Or at the very least that I would fall in love with you."

Okay. Now he has my interest. The *love* word.

Are men just interested in play things, someone to roll around with until they get bored and decide to do something else? Most women are thinking about the future from the minute they met a guy. Trying to figure out how things are going to play out and how it might work long term. I want to believe that when I am with someone it will work out in some way, shape or form over the long haul.

"I don't get it. So, now you have feelings for me, you are going to leave?"

"That's the plan."

We had an enjoyable holiday season and I admit, I do like this man, despite his interest in appearances and his obsession with money and fame. He acts as if he has unlimited funds and he takes me to very nice places. His obsession with money makes me wonder if he really has any.

After he leaves for New York, we do the long distance relationship thing. He leases an apartment on the east side in Manhattan and on his first night there he phones and describes the view over the Central Park at sunset. Within weeks, his calls are consumed with frustration; the world is not stopping to take notice. Why can't they see what I see, he asks? I really deserve more. I'm entitled to it.

About a month after his departure, I fly out to visit him. It's my first trip to Manhattan .

At the airport, a woman dressed in furs and

ordering her chauffer around, took a long look at me, "Honey," she said, "you are a sight for sore eyes. You look like you're from another era."

I smiled and thanked her. I was wearing a mid-length dress and stilettos.

"I remember when this city had the likes of you all the time," she said, straightening her hat and walking away.

Mr. New York was waiting in a cab. He opened the door, pushed me and as I fell in, he was all over me. Oh yes!

I was excited and thrilled about everything, the skyline, the people on the street, the Brooklyn Bridge, and having foreplay in a cab. It was spectacular. We went directly to Kevin's fabulous east side apartment for fun and play.

Later, we walked Central Park and had dinner at an exciting restaurant. Kevin was in his element, Manhattan, and it seemed the entire world was his. He took me to several clubs where we listened to music, drank champagne and talked about everything.

We met his cousin, Cameron, and his fiancée, Stephanie, for dinner the next night and I began to learn more about Mr. New York. I saw a jealous or envious side I'd never seen. Cameron was self confident and natural, he seemed to have it all, and was living on a "substantial inheritance" according to Kevin.

As we visited, Kevin would lean back and make snide comments about Cameron into my ear. 'Cameron sits on his ass all day and doesn't do a damn thing.' 'If Cameron didn't have all that money he wouldn't have a friend in the world.'

It was evident Mr. New York admired his cousin and wanted his approval. After dinner and drinks, Cameron looked at me,

"I always wondered why Kevin wasn't interested in dating someone here," he said, now leaning over the table towards me, "but now I know why. You are truly beautiful."

"Thank you."

Stephanie was peeved at his comment.

Mr. New York beamed, his rich cousin liked me. I was glad Kevin was proud of me but I down deep felt like a choice cut of steak.

If I felt like a piece of meat that night, the next day I felt as if I were an entire side of beef. We took a cab to Cameron's father's recording studio located on the top floor in a line of tall buildings where popular music had been composed and recorded since the early 1960s. I can't remember how many men I was introduced to but none of them really saw me, except for my legs, my ass and my breasts. A few did look at my face. They all lined up along one hallway smiling and smirking as Kevin parade his wild and exotic animal past them. I can just imagine what a black woman might have felt like standing on the auction block during slave times. If the men's eyes had hands there wouldn't have been a single place they had not touched, fondled and searched. Kevin couldn't have been prouder, pushing out his chest. He should have put me on a leash; I was his possession.

That night, Kevin was in excellent spirits and we had drinks at one club, dinner at another, then went from one club to the next as he showed me off to his friends and the world.

The next day, I escaped the petting zoo and went shopping. If I was going to be the main attraction I wanted to look stunning. At Saks Fifth Avenue, I went from one department to the next, from one floor to the next and then back again. I was searching for something special but classic so I could wear it for a while. I immediately picked a smashing pair of red leather pants that fit like a glove, and a classic cashmere coat that was to die for.

I discovered two beautiful outfits after trying on dozens. One was an elegant black dress and the other a sexy party dress. They were perfect and fit my body as if they were tailored for me. The staff was great and treated me as if I were royalty. I had never had an experience like it.

"I'll take them - both," I told the sales person.

"Yes, ma'am. I'm sure you will be very happy with these." After taking my credit card, she handed me an album containing their upcoming spring collection. As I thumbed through it, I realized I was on the Designer floor. Oh my god! I had gone from department to department, from floor to floor, not realizing where I ended up. I felt flushed as if I might panic. What if my credit card is denied! I hadn't even looked at the price tags! I wanted to dash away, to escape but I couldn't - they had my credit card. What is wrong with me?

After a long time, the sales person returned wearing a smile. My credit card had been accepted, but I still did not know how much I spent.

"Would you like us to deliver your purchase to your home address?"

"No, thank you. I'll take them with me."

Without looking, I signed the credit card receipt, took my dresses and left. Once on the sidewalk I got the courage to see what the price was. Four thousand dollars! For an instant I felt weak as if I might collapse, then I figured, hey, it's a one time deal and a shopping spree I'll never forget! Next time, I'll make sure to find out what floor I'm on first.

At Mr. New York's apartment I modeled my new purchases. The first thing he asked was, "How much?"

I told him the story and he insisted I take them back. He liked the black dress but thought the party dress was just too showy.

"If you keep that one," he told me, "it will be for my eyes only."

Sure. At that price, I'm showing the world.

The morning of my departure, we took a carriage through Central Park. It was beautiful and the park was filled with people strolling and walking their dogs, and the skyscrapers made the urban forest all the more stupendous by contrast. I had had such a great time I didn't want to leave. When he asked me about it, I cried. Damned tears! They'll betray a woman every time.

As he was comforting me, the carriage frightened a flock of pigeons and they suddenly took flight in a whirl wind of wings and light.

"Wouldn't it be something if one of them shit on our head?" Kevin said, jokingly.

At that exact moment, I felt a ker-plop on my head.

"I think a pigeon just shit on my head."

Sure enough, a good sized pigeon dropping nested in my red hair. We laughed and laughed and then I cried. Pigeon dropping or not, I didn't want this fairytale to end.

Back home, we talked on the telephone often and every month or two he flew to see me or I went to see him. When he was in Salt Lake City all he did was complain, there was nothing that satisfied him - except perhaps me. He hated the place and compared it to Manhattan at every turn. If you weren't here, he once told me, I'd never come back.

At first, I just listened to his complaints and agreed with them. I mean, trying to compare a small provincial ultra-conservative religious community with the Big Apple is impossible. But after a while, I started to take his constant insults personally. After all, I was supportive of his New York lifestyle, I worked hard to pay the bills when he was in town, and I tried to be everything he wanted me to be. I wanted him to enjoy his time here.

In part, the source of his foul moods was that his New York dream of becoming an important player in the music industry was not working out. While he talked endlessly of his musical knowledge, he was neither a musician, nor he didn't compose or write music. And, he definitely did not have a voice.   I wasn't sure where he would fit in but I just took him at his word. He knew he would soon make his mark. Who am I to castigate anyone for trying making their dream into reality.

Another major problem, he was running out of money. A year had past and not one of his grand plans materialized.

He started asking for money. I dropped everything and sent it to him. Sometimes, I paid his credit card bills and occasionally the rent on his east side apartment. Secretly, I was hoping that one day the favor would be returned. I've made this mistake before, more than once. I began to find fault with him. He is two inches shorter than I am when I'm barefoot - and in heels, I tower over him. I hated his teeth but loved his hair.

Kevin wanted to start at the top. Instead of working his way up, taking whatever position might be available and then making himself indispensable, he refused. He also refused help from his uncle and Cameron, insisting his talent and ability warranted a top executive's position. I guess he wanted to start at the top and then go stratospheric. I see a lot of that kind of star struck behavior these days.

I hired a twenty-year-old stylist and she informed me she wouldn't be staying long. Why, I asked? She confidently told me she was going to be famous soon and would be gone. What is going to make you famous, I enquired? She looked puzzled, "I don't know yet. I just know I'm going to be famous."

When I traveled to New York, I made sure I had plenty of cash and my cards were not maxed out. We always had a great time going to clubs and restaurants and the theatre - and it was always on me. I packed my most stunning outfits and bought a few new things there so I could be his "eloquent poster child." He paraded me before everyone, his friends, family and business associates. We often arrived a little late for social engagements so he could take my arm and have me prance back in forth for their approval. Kevin was very concerned about me looking good, although he didn't care what I looked like in bed. I was his prize, consolation for the deals he didn't get, the record industry champion he was not.

"I miss you so much," Kevin told me one night on the phone. "I just wish I had something of you here - to remind me of you."

"Like what?"

"Well, you know it's my thirtieth birthday soon and what I would like is a nude painting of you."

"You would!" I said. "Okay."

I guess many men fantasize about having a painting or an artistic photograph of their lover in the nude. I had never considered the idea until he asked and I had my reservations. After all, I was a mother and while I looked good in clothing, the idea of being naked intimidated me.

A client of mine is a well known oil painter and I asked him if I could commission him to do the painting. He seemed a bit embarrassed and at first declined, saying he didn't do nudes. After I pleaded he reconsidered and took Polaroid's of me standing and sitting and laying nude on a couch. We picked the one we thought was best for the painting and he went to work. I would strongly advise anyone thinking of doing something like this to first spend six months working out with a personal trainer at the gym. It was a humbling experience. On the day of the photo shoot, I conditioned my hair, did my nails, had a pedicure and a complete body scrub to make my skin luminous. It is easy being sexy in clothes but without them, nothing looks as inviting.

I sent the expensive commissioned painting off to Mr. New York and anxiously waited for his response.

He called late one night a few days later. We

talked about our usual subject: him but he said noting about the painting.

"Well," I finally enquired, "did you get the birthday painting I sent?"

Silence. "Yeah, I got it."

"Well?"

"It's okay, I guess. Thanks. Not what I expected, but it's okay."

I was devastated. "What's wrong with it?"

"Nothing really. You're just so much more beautiful than the painting. It doesn't look at all like you."

"Oh," I said slowly, "You didn't like it."

"It was okay."

Kevin then went right on with another story about his plight and didn't mention it again. I was angry and hurt. I spent considerable time, money and good-will on this present - that he requested - and got nothing but a lukewarm dissing for it.

As time passed, the calls became fewer and fewer. When he did call, he wanted money. He always called it a loan but since he never made a single attempt to pay anything back, the word loan is probably not accurate. I did, however, get many thank you comments and you're the best!

Last time I saw Mr. New York it was Valentine's

Day and I flew out to see him. He took me to one of the finest restaurants in the city and when the bill came, he took my credit card and handed it to our waiter. They both smiled at me. I felt like a he was a male whore and I was having to pay for my own dates.

When I left New York that time, I knew I would never be back - to see Kevin at least. That is the last time I saw him. He still calls occasionally on an irregular basis, and he is still trying to start at the top and go up from there.

I am left with the hope that I won't make the same mistakes again.

Chapter Sixteen
Dating clients

Kent, the Cabin Man, is back. I wonder how many people have a relationship like ours? For two people who have never been together as a couple, our level of intimacy is deep and abiding. Kent no longer lives here but we see one another when he visits. It is what it is. We are no longer sexually intimate but we have great foreplay. It has opened my eyes to a kind of sexual intimacy I've never had before. It is the ultimate in safe sex - and a lot of fun - at least for me. Our friendship is now in its eighth year.

Since he doesn't live here, and he wants no commitment, it's just an unusual intimate relationship. I never feel like I am cheating when I see other men, but I've had Kent in my life for longer than anyone. Perhaps that is the secret, distance equals the freedom we both need.

We talk often on the telephone. We agreed recently that ours was a strange and unique situation. I value Kent because I can tell him anything and he will not judge or lecture me. He listens and makes valued advice. He is wise and tender and listens to whatever I have to say. He is the best story teller I have ever known.

I know he cares about me and we have developed into exceptionally close friends - the physical, sexual stuff is a bonus. But, when he asked me about other men not long ago, I realized his feelings are more than friendship.

He invited me to fly up to his hometown for a weekend then, as an afterthought, asked me about other men in my life. I gave him the rundown of the men I was dating and I told him there were others, too. He was going to call me back with flight information but the weekend came and went and I heard nothing from him. I was disappointed and didn't know what to think.

A week later, he called and admitted being hurt about my response to other men question.

"You asked me a question, Kent. I just answered it. If you didn't want to hear about my dates, why did you ask?"

"I understand, Tonya. But it hurts."

I really don't think he does understand.

"Did you think I have been sitting around for all these years not seeing anyone?"

Silence.

Never Date a Client

The first rule in being a stylist is, never date

clients. The second rule is, NEVER date clients.

When Lee called I assumed he wanted an appointment.

"No," he says, "I am calling for something else."

"Oh, what would that be?"

"Are you seeing any one?"

"No."

"Okay good! Would you like to go to a play with me on Friday night?"

"Sure."

"I'm delighted."

I hung up and reminded myself, you have rules. DO NOT DATE CLIENTS! Okay, now what? I don't think I'm even interested in Lee. What was I thinking? I really wasn't thinking, I just answered yes. Maybe I am interested in him, subconsciously.

Lee is an interesting character - an eccentric. Well mannered, well read and with a calmness I usually don't see in men or women. Very polite and courteous, he is sincere and truly means it. I was intrigued. He is handsome and at least six-feet-something. His height is great for me, in heels lesser men feel intimidated as I tower above them. I don't mind but I suspect they do. Since I'm talking myself into this invitation, Lee has the most beautiful see through eyes. Sometimes green, other times brown. His eyebrows are thick with an arc similar to Marilyn Monroe, if only he shaped them.

Lee is always in character - but which character is the real question. He works as an accountant or CFO of a mid-sized corporation but his wardrobe is strictly thrift store chic. He has a penchant for mechanic or janitorial shirts and trousers. I often wondered if he wanted to be someone else. His worker shirts were always embossed with names: Burt, Vern or my favorite, Earl. He is the Starch King and has his own industrial style ironing board.

Our first date was really fun. The play was excellent and we had dinner at an upscale bistro downtown. I love to dress up so I wore a classy and elegant outfit I bought in LA.

"I just can't figure you out," Lee said, taking a sip of wine.

"What do you mean?"

"You're beautiful and successful but you don't have a man in your life."

"I've had a few relationships, like you."

"Oh, not me. I had a girlfriend in high school, my first love, then I got married. Not so much to talk about."

"What happened to the marriage?"

"Oh, you know. Someone always takes a fall. In my case, my wife started cheating - who knows why - and after a few affairs, I just couldn't forgive and forget anymore."

"A *few* affairs?"

"I don't know how many. One is enough. She just wasn't happy and the truth is, neither was I."

Lee looked straight into my eyes with his calm gaze. "It's an age old story. We got married too soon, you know, the church and the pressure to find someone and make a life. We had the boys and then everything started falling apart. On the outside, we looked like we had everything, but appearances are always wrong."

Oh, I know about appearances. Every Mormon family looks like the Cleavers, perfect in every way - on the outside. The Mormon Church pushes the boys and girls together as soon as they graduate from high school. It is a control thing, they get everyone matched up as soon as possible - pump out as many kids as possible and then they have you. Stuck! The woman can't get out because she is a Mother, with house full of kids; and, the man can't get out because he is a Father, and has to work his tail off to support everyone. It is nothing for a woman in her thirties to be all worn out, after having six or eight kids.

As we talked, I realized I had been in this

situation before. Another date, another man. We go out, start to date, have fun for a while, then the newness wears off and the problems start. We soon find out what the other person has been hiding, usually insecurity or money problems or something else. I start paying for everything and the man who wanted to take care of me really can't because he is a loser who can't find a job or keep the one he has.

"After I found out she was sleeping around," Lee went on, "I took the Book of Mormon and all the church teachings out into the backyard and burned them in the Webber. "

I laughed and laughed.

"Can you believe it?" he went on, shaking his head, "I was raised in the church and believed all their bull shit for so many years."

I could just picture him in the backyard, pouring lighter fluid all over his Book of Mormon and lighting it up. The Mormon neighbors are watching and before the fire is out, they are on the phone to the bishop.

Back at my house, he drops me off and we kiss.

A few days later, he drops by my house just as I was cleaning up a broken glass out on the patio. After I finished, we cruised the thrift shops, searching for work shirts and anything we could find.

Later that week, I receive an envelope in the

mail at work. It contained a poem:

YOU'RE BEAUTIFUL
Velvet eyes are a part of me
Sunset smiles and secret tears
Time my life to a fallen leaf
Watch the spring in all its plumage

Beautiful like the stars at night
Twist and turn like the dawn
Beautiful like the moon at night
Ducks and dives into the sea

Curtains drawn you'll miss the light
Your dawning spell will be broken
Vanished days are hard to find
Half-life dreams will not be worth much
You're Beautiful like the stars at night
Twist and turn like the dawn
Beautiful like the moon at night
Ducks and dives into the sea
(Mojave 3)
Lee

I'm impressed, no one had ever written a poem
for me. What a wonderful compliment - so artistic

and *I* was the subject. At the same time, I started to sense some strange distance or some odd differences in our styles. Could he really shake off his Mormon background like a dog shaking off a bad case of fleas? Since the poem arrived at the salon, I let the rest of the office read it.

One of the girls made a comment, "What is it you are not sure about? If I got a letter like that I would be all over him."

Okay, coming from a Mormon girl who wants nothing more than to be married and have tons of kids right away; and does everything but have intercourse, because it's within the rules, I can see her point. Today you can do everything - blow jobs and anal sex - and as long as you don't have penetration, you are not really having sex. I think not. Anyway, she is the office tease and a bit on the jealous side. So, I couldn't see what she was seeing.

"I have never received anything like this before." I admitted. While Lee was always a gentlemen and seemed so normal, I started getting the vibe that although he had burned all his religious paraphernalia, he was still a little prudish, formal and reserved. Mormon men are called Elders and Lee acted a like an elder.

One night at my house, a few of my friends

came by when Lee was there. The conversation turned to sex. Mika, my best friend, has been married for a long time and, Sally, who was recently divorced, decided to give her some pointers on sex.

Lee was standing behind the bar.

"The best way to keep a man is to give him the most memorable blow jobs ever!"

Straight faced Mika asked, "How do you so that? I'm not very good at them. What's your secret?"

I was having a hard time keeping a straight face. Lee was listening but I'm not going to chance taking a look to see his expression.

As serious as she could be, Sally elaborated on her technique. She even gave a demonstration. Holding her hands together as if grasping a penis, she opened her mouth and went up and down a few times, then stuck her tongue out and simulated licking.

Now wait a minute, I'm thinking, that doesn't work on every one! I decide not to pipe up because I didn't want to give Lee ideas.

"I think I might give that a try," Mika said, "I'll let you know how it works."

Lee seemed cool and unemotional. This is not the way a man acts when women are simulating blow jobs in his presence; the least he could have done is make a joke or snide comment. His response did not have the ring of truth. I just had to laugh - to myself, of course - but I wondered, is this something you want someone you are dating to hear?

After a delightful get-away trip to Seattle, I received the second lovely poem from Lee. Our weekend in Seattle was just what I needed. Owning a business and being a single parent takes so much energy and time, I was thrilled when he asked if I wanted to go. He took care of all the details, even reserving a hotel on the grounds of a famous winery. I love wine and he did it for me.

On our arrival, I informed him that we weren't going to be having sex. He just stood there and said, "I know." After all, I hadn't decided if I liked him really. At the same time, Lee had made comments about his inability to get and keep an erection occasionally. I thought he was joking at first, I mean, the way the man looked at me when I wore something revealing or sexy, I knew he was interested in it.

We hiked and walked the shoreline and took a ferry to the islands. On the second night, we both drank too much and started making-out. It went to the next level. We were laying on a couch when suddenly he jumped up and said he couldn't do it. What do you mean, I asked? For some reason, he told me, "I can't get an erection!"

The trip was soothing and restful. We ate at nice restaurants and as always, Lee, was a consummate gentleman. It was starting to irk me. He was too perfect, too much of a gentleman, too mild and agreeable.

A day or two after returning, I received the poem.

HER NAME WRITTEN IN COLORS I'VE FELT

In black, she holds my arm for the first time.
I react like a nervous boy.
In purple, I see her kneel over broken glass.
I collect a piece to hold her reflection.
In red, I see her smile as she sits like a child.
I hear stories of her as a girl.
In violet, the sun and she color the sky.
Her dress like a flag falls to the floor.
In darkness, I hold her and understand why.
She like the light allows color to thrive.
In hues of color that fill my heart, I watch as I fall in
Love.
In shades of color held by her frame, I fall in love as I
write her name.

Each color represented a date and what I was wearing. I knew then I was in trouble. Lee wanted to marry me and I wasn't ready for that kind of commitment. I guess I had been looking for someone to take care of me, to treat me with respect and honor me, someone who was honest and thoughtful and considerate and kind. Now, I had him, a true boy scout of America and I wanted to get away. What's wrong with me?

I decided to try to like him and see what developed.

Over the next few months, we saw each other a couple times a week and it was fun. He was interesting, quirky and had a great sense of humor. While the wow factor was minimal, the reliability quotient was high. I knew that Lee would always be steady and dependable. After unsuccessful tries with bad boys, most women pick someone like Lee, trustworthy, sincere and well, uninspiring.

At Christmas time, I decided I would get him a few inexpensive gifts that I thought he might like: a book, a Bonsai tree and a few male trinkets. Sitting on my living room couch he gave me some very nice individually wrapped gifts. A candle and candle holder. He knew I like to cleanse my thoughts of the day's stress by lighting a scented candle. Then a small, exquisitely wrapped box.

Inside, sat a ruby and diamond ring. It was stunning and I was stunned - almost paralyzed at the sight of it. I couldn't move or talk. I had never received a ring from a man - ever. I sat there looking at it like some terracotta statue. I had dreamed of the moment someone would give me a diamond and here it was - but I couldn't do or say anything. I just stared at it. Later, I wondered if I had been putting out the marriage and ring vibe, but concluded I hadn't.

A month later, when everything was calm and enjoyable, I finally told him, "Thank you for the ring. No one has ever given me a ring before."

He smiled and said he understood. We dropped the subject and never spoke about it again.

I knew Lee had fallen in love with me but I felt the same as I did at the beginning: he was a great guy but the sparks and the passion were just not there. I wondered how anyone could like me as much as he did. He would do anything for me and while that gave me some deep comfort, it made me feel uncomfortable at the same time.

Without any words passing between us, I knew that our one year anniversary date was the big one: time to get intimate. He sent a letter penned in pink ink and embossed with a beautiful row of roses at the top, it read:

You and I sitting in an enormous bathtub surrounded
by a thousand candles. I wash your hair, caress your
feet, and hold you in my arms as the warmth of the
water takes us.

As you lay on the bed and the candle's light dances on
your skin, I shower your body with rose petals. We lay
expectant of what is to happen. We kiss and become
one as our limbs embrace. I become lost in the beauty
as I explore every inch of your form.

Time begins to fold in on itself and repeat as the
foreplay of this night proceeds. You achieve orgasm
easily in this precursor to sex. I realize enlightenment
as I witness the pleasure displayed on your face. We
begin to make love as music plays to the rhythm of our
movement. You lean over to kiss my neck as you sit
over me. My hands trace the contours of your chest,
your waist, and come to rest on your hips. We both call
to God as we climax and continue.

We lay facing each other and your arm moves across
my back. I touch your face with the back of my hand
and feel the soft texture of your skin melt against mine.

The candles flicker and go out. We fall asleep not
needing to dream.

Love Lee

In small lettering, he inscribes in gray ink:

This is my fantasy. I know you have questions and concerns given my problem to perform sexually. I want to let you know that these problems are recent and not indicative of my past. For whatever reason, nature has been playing games with me. As you know, I have been seeing my doctor to try and fix this malady. What I ask is that you give me a chance to start over with our sexual relationship. I can't promise anything, but I will do whatever I can to regain your desire. You are so beautiful and sexually attractive to me, and I want you to feel the same for me.

Let me know if you would be receptive to spending this Friday night with me. I have attached details to a few rooms at Snowbird. If this plan is alright with you, I can call and see if any of these rooms are available.

Do I talk myself into liking him? I knew I wasn't in love with him. I always felt as if something was missing. He used to take pieces of my hair and put them in his pocket. He told me, 'I want to carry you with me.'

I invite Mika, my friend, and her daughter, Brickel, to go with us. Of course, Jonny would be there, too - he loves hotels and room service. I guess

I was trying to shield myself, to surround myself with other people so it didn't get too intense.

Before we head up the canyon, Lee had a minor car accident. Lee is a diabetic, his blood sugar was low and he had bumped a car at an intersection. He had his two boys and Jonny with him. I quickly left work and picked them up because the police were not going to let him drive. Lee was disoriented and strange. After arriving back at the salon, he mysteriously left while I was busy with a client.

His youngest son came in crying and wanted to use the phone. "What's wrong?"

"We aren't going. I need to call my mom to come and get me."

"Where's your Dad?"

"He's walking home."

"What?"

"He just left!"

I found him about a mile away.

"What are you doing?"

"Walking home."

I was annoyed and angry.

"Well, I'm heading up the canyon." I said loudly. "Are you coming with me or not."

He climbed in and together with the boys we drove silently up the canyon.

Once there, I was exhausted and Mika offered to cook dinner. Spaghetti is her master dish. She could tell I was tired and ready for bed. I ate and went straight to the master suite. The day had been filled with frustration and I wanted to be alone.

The next thing I know, Lee has laid down next to me and is running his hands all over me, fondling my breasts.

Annoyed, I asked him what he was doing.

"I only want to touch your skin."

"I'm too tired, Lee. It has been a long day."

He pouted for a minute, then like a dejected child got up and left.

For most of the next day I slept and tried to avoid him. In the late afternoon, while he was doing something with the boys, I went to a small outdoor bar where a band was playing. I had one too many drinks and was drunk. Lee found me there. He didn't say a word but instead sat across from me and just looked at me with a smile on his face. He often sat and stared at me, it always made me uncomfortable.

A married client happened to be at the resort and saw us sitting together. He commented what an attractive couple we were together and asked if we were planning to get married.

Oh no!

Lee was thrilled but I gave my client the death-ray look when Lee was not watching.

The next week, I told Lee I didn't want to see him anymore. I finally faced my real feelings and realized he liked me a lot more than I liked him. I just wasn't fair to either of us. I couldn't talk myself into loving him.

He was angry.

"Am I not rich enough? Am I to skinny for you? Is there someone else?" The list went on.

The answer was none of the above. I told him I was claustrophobic. He didn't handle it well.

The truth is, I guess, I have my own commitment issues.

I felt bad for leaving Lee. It was fun to be with him but the butterflies were never there. I wish him well. It is never a good idea to date clients.

Chapter Seventeen
Unanswered questions

I have an urge for something, I'm just not sure
what it is. Relax, and put your mind at ease, I repeat
to myself. Unfortunately, this time it's not working.
I have no desire to get smacked in the face again. I
am sure it will happen - life comes up behind us and
whamo! I'm getting really tired of repeating mistakes
and I want a change in my life. I never imagined at
this point in my life I'd still be working this hard to
survive. I put a smile on everyday, hoping that today
it will be real. My neck hurts and needs attention.
My stomach is popping out and my throat seems
constricted.

I must be holding in some need or desire
that wants to get out. Our inner needs want to be
communicated, to know words, to be manifested, to
be dealt with. I'm feeling so tired of myself. I wish I
could call back all of the energy I've given away. I
could use it right now.

I had no idea my life would turn out the way
it has developed. I remember the early dreams of my
future, visions of an exciting new world. None of
those dreams even vaguely resemble today's reality.
Reality never matches our dreams or predictions or

desires. I feel I am in the middle of a maze, searching to find my way out, or the answer to the questions that seem to have no answer.

What is wrong with me? Why should I want out? I have a great relationship, Jonny seems to be doing well, business is as good as I can expect it, and I'm living in my dream house. What is this constant nagging dissatisfaction? Why does this feeling of being incomplete or of waiting for something to happen never go away?

My new house has everything I ever wanted! I should feel satisfied - but I'm not. Perhaps I'm still reeling from the real estate buying process. The constant questioning whether I was doing the right thing or not; whether I could afford it; worrying about what happens if I get sick and unable to pay the sizable mortgage. I battled the nagging idea that I couldn't think for myself, and I was petrified I might make the wrong decision. I've made some poor choices in the past and they all lined up and came back to haunt me. Every time I've thought something was the right choice, my life became more complicated, and more of a tangled, upside-down mess.

I thought, why not purchase your dream house? It was as if the house was calling to me, saying - Tonya, I'm yours, please buy me. Look, I have everything you want. I went to see my astrologer: it was in the stars. I went to see the palm reader: it was in my future. I was drawn to it like the visions of a fabulous new product line, or the dreams of a man who would always love me and never leave me. The house made me feel as if I was home. Perhaps, that is what is missing. A house is sometimes not a home.

Luckily, I have a real relationship with a mature and responsible man, but it frightens me a little. Admittedly, I've been drawn to men who weren't available or ready. It was no commitment but fun. As soon as someone wanted or offered more I found the nearest exit and disappeared. I've enjoyed my freedom, but of course, the gnawing emptiness never stopped. I've always wanted more. Will the gnawing ever cease, will I ever be satisfied?

Every time I think my business is doing well, I get smacked in the face again! Last time, I bought the Jaguar to reward myself, but the women stylists decided I was some kind of slaveholder and living the high life off the sweat of their brow. It didn't take too long before I had an insurrection and they all walked out - going down the street to support another salon owner.

So, once again, I was in business crisis mode.

Work harder, work harder. Don't depend on anyone. Do it yourself. These are my work mantras. They saved me time and again. Unfortunately, I don't have the endless supply of energy I had ten years ago. I need help and I hate asking for it. I can't ask for it. I may go down with the ship.

And now, I have my dream house and a not so dreamy mortgage. The strange thing is, for the first time I don't want to work. I want to be home. I want to be a mom. Would this be considered a defeat for a card carrying career woman? The independent woman now wants to be home cooking, cleaning, making cookies. Right. I would like to have some guests and elaborate parties. We would drink wine and share in each others lives. Oh god, I can't believe I just said that.

Have I lost my mind? What am I thinking? I want to work less? Leave the career I have worked so hard to attain? Few have an idea of what it is like to be a stylist in this city. Not only are the people terminally cheap, they expect to be treated like celebrities. I wonder if real celebrities spend their free time clipping coupons?

I have to find a way to make an income that will take me to retirement and give me a fun, fulfilling life. Sure. Is this what men call a mid life crisis? They work for twenty years, have something tangible to show for it but arrive at a point where they are so bored and dead to life, they want to chuck it all and sign-on as a deckhand on a sailing schooner? I've never been the stay at home mom. I have always been the bread winner. How can I keep myself going with this unrelenting routine for the next twenty years?

If I were finding a cure for childhood cancer, would I be fulfilled? If I were a philosopher and book author with people clamoring to sit and listen to me, would I be fulfilled? If I had a solid partner in love and life, a man who would take care of me, like so many other woman have, would I have a fulfilling life? I don't know.

How many people are truly happy? Most of us just seem to be going through the motions. I read that the Yucci Indians in Mexico believe that we Americans are not truly awake or conscious, even though we are walking around and appear to be awake. Are we all just material zombies? Are we missing the true meaning of being alive?

Have I wasted my life on things that don't matter? I now realize my son doesn't care to spend time with me. After all, he is a teenager. What would someone his age ever want to do with their mother? That would be the most uncool thing ever.

Have I missed the opportunity to be a mom? Is it too late to spend a day making Christmas cookies? Could I decorate my house and actually have holiday parties? Can I see this as being a part of my future? Is this something that will never happen? Am I destined to just live life day by day bored to death by routine and every day occurrences?

I've been working to get past my past, but now
I'm worried about Arthur's past. I am at the airport
and everywhere I turn I see blondes. They pop up one
after another as I make my way to my gate. I bumped
into one coming out of the bathroom, another near the
escalator, and still another coming at me head-on along
the concourse. Is someone or something trying to tell
me something?

It reminds me of when Arthur and I first started
dating. Arthur took me to strip clubs almost every
weekend. I guess it was alright in the beginning, I had
never really been to any strip clubs before.

Almost every stripper was a bottle blonde.
At first, I wondered how these young women got so
depressed they felt a need to take their clothes off
and show their bodies for money. Some were single
mothers and needed money to support their children.
A few were college students paying for tuition and
training for professional careers. I learned some started
stripping part time and going to college, but decided to
strip full time because they could make more money in
two hours taking their clothes off than working eight
hours with a college education. Of course, no one stays

young for long, and from what I hear, strippers start looking hard and old quickly.

The first time we went to a strip club we met friends of Arthurs, and sat in a booth near the front. We were in our seats less than a minute when Arthur pointed out a stripper and proudly informed me he once dated her. I'm really not thrilled to see her, but what the hell, here she comes. She is attractive, tall and thin. She is half my size or smaller. She is chocolate colored and really had no figure at all, just straight up and down. I am thinking to myself, 'What the hell did he bring me here for? I am not that thin!'

She looked as if she hadn't seen food this decade, like an Ethiopian refugee. I felt a bit awkward and slightly sick. I wanted to leave.

Eventually, we left and I couldn't wait to get home. It was not my idea of a good time. I still wonder why he takes me to those places; he has to know I don't enjoy it. Do men think their partner wants to see what they have slept with?

Not long ago, we went to a night club down town to celebrate a friend's birthday. We took a booth where we could people watch. We noticed how most of the women were blondes - colored all of them. It was like the commercial where all the models are blondes prancing around and then they throw off their wigs -

but in this situation they were not wigs.

Arthur had made a passing comment about his ex wife and how it was strange he never ran in to her. Sure enough, a minute later, she walked through the door.

Before he could get a word out, I saw a woman enter and my first impression was she looked like a clown. She was wearing a ton of garish make-up , a strange outfit and a big floppy hat. She looked a bit plastic - as in plastic surgery - and I thought, tits on a stick. It was as if she had a face lift and her face was about to crack. Before I could make a comment, Arthur pipes up, "Oh my God, that's Allie!"

Okay. Once again a tall, wafer-like, anorexia-looking blonde. Arthur kicked back in his seat like he was in shock. I knew he really wanted to run in to her. I can't say he wanted to be with her, but he was curious about what happened to her and especially her son. Arthur had fathered the boy until the marriage ended. Sure enough, she spotted him and came prancing over to introduce her new fiancée and soon to be husband - number four.

Arthur asks about the Italian guy - the one she was sleeping with when they were married. She narrows her eyes and purses her lips - she doesn't want to talk about it. After they left, he said "Gawd, I feel sorry for the poor sap if he is going to marry her."

I felt as if I need to go on a diet - now! A diet that will make my body half the size and weight. I am not insecure about how I look but every woman in Arthur's past is tiny. What is he doing with me? The couple with us felt uncomfortable for me. The woman sensed I was troubled and looked at everyone at the table, stopping at Arthur, and in a loud voice tells everyone how she can't believe how beautiful I am. "She should be a model," she said. Thank god for her.

I simply said thank you. After all, I didn't have on a stitch of make-up, except for a bit of lip stick. I just couldn't escape the feeling that I should lose some poundage.

Later at home, the last thing on my mind was sex, which is strange because it is usually the first thing on my mind. I wonder, am I just a phase? Am I just someone helping Arthur along the way until the next tiny blonde comes into his life? The thought of it makes me sick.

A few days later, I'm stuck at the car dealership needing a ride. I call Arthur but no answer. Strange, he always answers. I called again an hour later.

"Hello."

"Where have you been?" I ask. "I called but no one answered. Where are you?"

"My old house."

"What old house, the one you sold?"

"Yeah. I got a call from Allie's parents who…"

"What?" I interrupted.

"They wanted to talk to me, so I drove over. We had a very interesting conversation."

Apparently, Arthur's ex-wife was now a drug addict and her parents were desperate for help - from anyone. So, they called Arthur. He had fathered her son for several years when they were married after the biological father disappeared. Arthur cared about the boy and was interested in helping if he could. Funny how you don't see someone for years and in one week you run into them at an old haunt, and then their parents call and ask for help. I wonder if I'm getting the entire story or just bits and pieces.

All of this is just too much for me, I am reminded of Brad and his crazy girlfriend who tried to break into my house. Suddenly, I realize my past is coming back to visit me. I can just image now that Allie, Ms. Tits on a Stick, Ms. Drug Addict, will show up at my place now that Arthur is living with me. Oh God! I don't bring my ex's around and I don't want Arthur's hanging around either. So now what? He's going to father his ex-wife's son? What does that entail? Her hanging around at my house?

I try to let my past go so I might find a new future. Why are these incidents looking so familiar from the past? I've helped a lot of people but I'm not interested in being involved in saving someone else - especially not his ex-wife or her son. Help yourself, I say.

My stomach is upset and empty, like the divorce diet sensation. I feel my throat constricting, choking. I'm holding back tears. Why do I feel this way? I wish this sensation would just go away. I have lost my luster. It's as if I constantly have allergies. May be I am allergic to myself.

I asked Arthur once if he wished I would wear more make up, he said no. He likes to kiss and hug and it doesn't taste very good.

I seem to be the fall girl in my relationships. I help pick them up, put them on a constructive path and then let them go. Where do I fit? Is this pattern part of my demise? Do I just set myself up for this?

I went to a palm reader once and she told me in a past life I had been a mystical creature, a fairy, or even a mermaid. Men will want me, she said, but they could never have me. They would die pining away. Right.

Of all of them, Mister Cabin Man is probably

pining for me. He needs love to survive or he will die. He loved me with all of him - or so he said. He was everything and nothing all at once. I hope he is near the ocean, enjoying the waves washing in and out. I wish I could better understand what I found so enjoyable about him. I felt calm in his arms, and I didn't want to leave. I enjoyed his fragrance and how his body covered me - like a wonderful caressing blanket. I felt safe in his arms. I hated leaving in the morning.

He will never know how I felt about him. I wrote him a letter but never delivered it. I told him we needed to move forward or we need to end it. I wanted a relationship; I wanted to have someone to hold in the middle of the night. I need a nook to snuggle down into. He wasn't there for that and never would be.

Now, I have Arthur. He is the nook I so desire. Sometimes, I make him hold me when he would rather not. He gets hot and doesn't enjoy being sticky. I can understand but I need something, too. I would never take him to places where we conveniently run into my old lovers. It doesn't matter who I dated, and I'm not interested in running into them.

Arthur has no desire to be married, it costs to much to get divorced. It makes me realize I am on my own. I should let the silly fairytale go - the dream I love and hate at the same time. It doesn't happen like that anymore. Times have changed. Women make more money and wield more power; men are feeling more vulnerable and less willing to make a stand. Nothing lasts forever. I need to get back into my own skin again. I left it somewhere, discarding it like a comfortable, worn-out sweater. Now, I need it back.

Arthur said once, "I have never had any one love me as deeply as you." I wonder if he knows he never will? I ask him if he wishes he was sleeping with someone else from time to time. He answered, no, but I secretly think he means, yes. He doesn't want to hurt my feelings. He has hurt women in the past by lying to them to save their feelings.

I wish I could turn into a man, again. I mean, to be out for myself and no one else. It was fun for a while. It felt lonely at times but I didn't want to let anyone in. I was safe. I didn't need or want a man, except occasionally for companionship. Now, I sometimes would like to be a housewife. Cleaning, cooking, and being a mom. Yikes! Did I say that?

I wish I could see a new future just over the horizon. I would let go of everything blocking my inner self and just go for it. My true spirit lies beneath the illusions and the girlie dreams I possess. I want to call back my spirit; it disappeared years ago when I was pregnant. It has yet to resurface and breath in the new air. I was truly happy back then. I want to feel the weight of this sadness lifted.

I can only pretend to be happy for so long. I want to see the colorful painting of the dreams I have hidden within me come to pass.

I thought I was unattractive and undeserving for such a long time. Deep inside I wanted to be the best of the best, to associate with like minded people, to make a difference in the world. Back then, I found solace and comfort taking journeys of the soul - and *my horse Christopher* would carry me on these journeys. It was peaceful and I had the solitude I needed to let go of all the mean and hateful people around me. Where is *Christopher* now?

Chapter Nineteen
Airport

I'm doing a one day trip to give a seminar and then fly home tonight. The Salt Lake International Airport is filled with Mormons, they are saying farewell to a small group of young missionaries. Missionaries give up two years of their lives to preach the gospel and attempt to convert people to the church. You've seen them in your neighborhood. They travel by bicycle in twos, wearing black pants, white short sleeve shirts and ties. They ask if they can tell you about the true church of Jesus Christ of Latter Day Saints. Mormons are easy to spot since they all look the same; the same uniform, the same blonde hair, the same blue eyes, the same vacant look on their faces.

They wear name tags but when greeting other people, they call them brother or sister. Today's group of Mormons are a little different, they are converts to the church from Tonga or Samoa. They have taken Mormonism as their religion but haven't given up their cultural roots entirely. Unlike their American or European counterparts, they are big and broad and dark and have beautiful skin. Yet, they wear the same uniform and have the same vacant look plastered on their faces. We share the same space at the exact same time, but I don't think we exist on the same planet. They are somewhere else, or perhaps I am somewhere else.

At the boarding gate, I have an image of The Cabin Man and I boarding a flight for some exotic ocean destination. It must be one of those unfulfilled fantasies that float inside my silly little head sometimes. Cabin Man called this week. I hadn't heard from him in a year and out of the ether he dials me up. It was so good to hear his voice; I felt as if my legs might drop out from underneath me. He said he was going to be in town soon and asked to see me. I made an excuse and didn't answer. Seeing him will just cause an uproar inside me. He was not the first man I loved, but my heart has placed him in that first-love position. He possesses a magical and mystical place in my psyche. I guess it is his idea of romance and love that places him at the top of the list. I felt so safe with him, in his arms or just being near him.

I can no long take off my clothes and adorn my body with his hands of rapture. That was then and this is now. He was never afraid to touch me or to mold himself into me as we lay on his bed at the cabin. Our relationship is over and perhaps that is why he now resides on the pantheon of love and sexuality for me. The Gods are unattainable and the Cabin Man was unattainable. I am not going to share my body with him any more. I have Arthur now. I gave him seven years to decide if he wanted a relationship or to just leave it as it was - and by default he chose the latter. It was just what it was. He loves me, I am sure of it - I can see it in his eyes - but his longing is not as strong as his fear of being hurt - again. If he could just get over the pain of yesterday he might have a chance at today. Easy for me to say. I just cannot see him again.

Arthur makes me feel as if I am on the waiting list, too. I know it is not his intention and I think he is not really aware he is doing it, but he is afraid to move forward or he simply does not know how too. We need a way to construct a relationship without going down the same worn out and unworkable path - the one that always leads to heartache and financial disaster.

Two women have come and gone and when they left, they took everything he had. It was the old axiom that goes: "everything that is mine is mine, and everything that is yours is mine, too." Women need to stop doing that to men. Soon, good men will be unwilling to make a try again. Arthur is committed to not letting it happen again. I suspect it is one of the reasons he picked me. I make more money than he does and I have a history of being a self sufficient workaholic.

Sitting in my window seat, I am suddenly swept away by the world I once knew as a child. I guess my moment of *magic and glory* happened on that day I was sleigh riding. I went somewhere far, far away. To a place of peace and fulfillment, a place where I was whole and did not have to do anything to be that way. I was just who I was and it was right. There were no worries.

No worries, how would it be? Would someone actually come to the table and love and support me? Would they take care of me and make my life free of worries? Men always tell me they are attracted to my independence, but I feel it is a cop out because they are afraid. What does a man have to offer a women who is independent? Companionship? I say get a dog. Great sex? One in a million. I wasn't able to enjoy sex until I was in my late thirties. Why? The fear of becoming a single parent again. Once was enough and I was always afraid of sex after Jonny. It made it not so fun for me. I hated it.

I finally got over disliking sex when I started to see Arthur. He had been snipped, too. The thing that make me crazy with Arthur is his inability to let go of the negative impact of his past marriages, the financial havoc they created for him. He wants to hang on to the picture that the dueling experiences gave to him. The picture of a happy prosperous life that he so desired to live, contrasted by paying for a house he loved while his ex-wife lived in it with the man she had been sleeping with while he was away making money to support her.

The only thing I can see about the here and now is I am not entirely with him. I don't want to waste my time with someone that does not sees me or who sees someone else in their future. But, if this is how it's going to be, I can deal with it but I need to know!

Am I just there for a time, filling the empty space until someone else comes along? Is this the real deal? Is he as happy with me as I am with him? Does the feeling make him want me more? Or is he wanting to celebrate life with some one else? I don't have the anorexic body that I see him admire so. I am what I am. It bothers me when I see him drool over other women. Perhaps I should drool over a few men and see how he likes it. Fortunately, it really isn't my nature.

Out the airplane window I can see the moon. It is waning but a few days ago it was full and amazing. It was so bright and the night was so dark, a black void. The contrast of the light and darkness make things stand out so dramatically. Why am I with Arthur anyway? What am I to him really? Someone to have sex with until something better comes along? I feel I will never be thin enough, not for his liking. I want to have an ass to look at. To me, there isn't anything appealing about a woman that is so thin she doesn't have an ass to admire.

Chapter Twenty
Blue Luis

How can you be married or in a serious relationship and have lovers, too? If the marriage isn't any good why not end it so you are free and then pursue women or men or other relationships or sex or whatever it is you want and need? A few years ago, Blue Luis gave me some insight into these and other questions.

Blue Luis and I met at the daycare. He dropped his two kids off the same time I dropped Jonny and we became friends. He liked me from the start and told me so. He was a computer geek without the geek-part; and, wore his hair in a mullet. He was handsome and not too tall. He worked out at the gym and his physique was perfect. His appearance was a big part of his self concept - isn't it that way for most of us? In a world where it's hard to believe in anything, I guess it makes sense to believe in what we see in the mirror - albeit a fanciful, non-objective illusion.

One morning, Blue Luis was waiting for me in the parking lot after I dropped Jonny off.

"What sign are you?" he asked.

"Gemini."

"I knew it! I just knew it!" he said shaking his

head in disbelief. "I don't know what it is, but I am always drawn to Gemini women!"

"Gemini's draw attention," I added.

"You do, anyway." He commented. "I always fall for Geminis."

"You can't be all bad, then."

Blue Luis is married and has two kids. He isn't happy but this was his second marriage and it is what it is. Once, when he was telling me about going out on his wife, I asked why he didn't just get a divorce, then he wouldn't have to lie.

"Have you ever lost everything?" he answered, downcast. "I have. My first wife got everything I worked for when we broke up. I can't afford to do *that* again."

"Why not make your marriage work, then?"

"We've tried. It just isn't going to work and I can't afford to start over again. My wife would get everything. That's the way it's done in America. Everything a woman acquires is hers, and everything the man acquires is hers, too."

I think Blue Luis was interested in me because I was unlike the other women he had been involved with. I even make more money than he does. According to him, I was a real turn-on. After hearing how he had lost everything, I understood better how he felt. He was paying child support and alimony. She got the house, car and everything else.

Brad had done a similar thing to me. He sat around for two years, I paid for everything and then before he left, he ripped me off and took everything. No wonder men are reluctant when it comes to a second or third marriages. Women have the upper hand in court.

Luis told me he had long fallen out of love. It was a business deal turned sour. According to him, his wife felt the same way but neither was ready to call it quits because they had a big house and a good deal of material wealth. They were willing to live in a pathetic and uncaring marriage so they could continue to drive nice cars, go on vacations and put on an outward show of prosperity and happiness.

Blue started showing up at the salon. He was funny and made me feel beautiful and desired. One day he told me, "Tonya, I love you."

"I know you do, Luis." I could tell that Blue Luis really did care for me. It was easy to see.

"Let's be lovers?"

"No."

"Why?"

"You're married for one thing," I started. "I've had that done to me - the betrayal and all. I have no interest in being the other woman. It isn't worth it."

"Why?"

"You don't know anything about women. I think you are cute, you have a lot going for you. I might like to be your lover but I would want more. You think if we were lovers, we would be lovers and that is all."

"So? Sounds good to me!"

"Women want to have a lover but NOT just a lover. We want a man, someone to have a relationship with, someone to build something with - like a life?"

"We could still be lovers?"

"You don't get it."

"Take our satisfaction and pleasure when we can get it."

"It's not that simple."

"Yes it is, if you let it be."

"You still don't understand."

"Look at it this way, Tonya. You and I may never be in this place again. The gods or spirits or the powers that be brought us here to be together. Even though it is not perfect, we need to grasp our opportunity and find out where it takes us."

"You are funny, Luis - romantic too. That was all very nice, a great line for women with little experience. Perhaps we were placed here just out of coincidence, chance. There is no meaning, except we are meant to be friends."

"But, you are a Gemini!"

"You still don't get it."

"I guess not."

When a client arrived at the salon, I introduced her to Blue Luis.

"Why do you call him Blue Luis?" she asked. "He doesn't look blue to me?"

"Oh, it's not the color blue," I replied, "it's just that I'm not interested in having a relationship with him."

Blue Luis smiled widely, and added, "She won't have me. I've been trying to get her to be with me. She just breaks my heart and makes me blue."

Everyone in the salon laughed.

"If you would only let me wine and dine you," he went on, "I know you would like it."

"No Luis." I responded, hand on hip, "You would like it and I would have to live with it."

"I'll fly you to New York for a shopping spree. How about that?"

No response.

"Or, what about Hawaii?"

Blue Luis does not know when to quit. He stands there arms open wide, a smile on his handsome face.

I turn and walk away.

A month later he is back. Always the same lines, always a gentleman. When I asked if he were still married he frowns and nods his head up and down. Seasons come and seasons go and Blue Luis shows up like a homing pigeon.

During one of Blue Luis absences, a young handsome man arrives. He is ten years younger than I am and looking for interesting places to plant his seeds. He has that sweet boy look, earnest and endearing.

He had a most disarming smile. When I realized he was not there for services of the salon, I assumed he wanted a job. As we talked, he kept smiling and blushing and acting embarrassed and unable to say what he really wanted.

I shook my head when he left, not knowing any more then about why he stopped by than when he arrived. Perhaps he was high on something, I concluded. Later, he called and invited me out for a glass of wine. Sure, I said.

We met at a nearby watering hole. He was free of responsibilities and was following his whims wherever they took him. Oh, to be young and unencumbered with the pressures of adulthood. He was easy to talk to but continued to smile and blush as if embarrassed.

"Are you looking for a job?" I asked.

"I can't work for you," he told me flatly.

"Why?"

"I'm attracted to you and I'm afraid I wouldn't get anything done."

"Really?" I said, laughing.

"Really. I did come by the salon looking for work but as soon as I met you I knew that wasn't going to happen."

Later, I took the boy home and we had some fun. It was a first for me, being with someone so much younger. He was really a boy - trying to find his way into manhood. What wasn't a first for me was the Tiny Weenie business. Why are men so concerned about the size of their penis? Men need to know that women aren't always thinking about size - well, maybe some of the time. The real concern should be, does it work or not. If it does, don't worry about size. If it doesn't work, that is a problem. Most women think it's them, that they were a turn off rather than being a turn-on.

The boy and I had fun for a while. He paid attention to my schedule and never wanted to come over when he knew I was busy. I saw him on and off in-between other dates and I realized he was just there because he liked sex and some fun. He didn't have to be responsible for anything, I took care of that. He came and went, sometimes showing up after months and telling me stories of his adventures roaming the country. It didn't matter to me, the sex was fun - even though it was not *that* good - and I guess it satisfied my curiosity about younger men.

Chapter Twenty-One
Ted Bundy

Before getting involved with Arthur, Nancy and I decide to meet for a glass of champagne. She was recently divorced and has a son three years younger than Jonny. She is new to the dating game and since most of our female friends are now married, we have formed a bond: we like to go out for drinks or stay in and eat microwave popcorn, watch chick-flicks and drink wine.

Our girl friends don't seem to find the same enjoyment they once did going out with the girls. Now, when they find time for a girl's night out, all they do is watch the clock and act nervous. As soon as they arrive, they are thinking about leaving. I suspect it's their husband's worrying about them being out with single women - my god, we might influence them to have sex with some random stranger. It could be that they have real lives now - complete with jobs, husbands, kids, bills to pay and mutual insecurities. Whatever.

I arrived at the lounge at River's before Nancy so I sat in a booth, ordered a glass of Champagne, scanned the television, and watched people arrive for dinner. I savor this alone time, and my champagne.

A man sitting across the room is watching me. Now, he is up and coming over.

"Hi, my name is Rory."

"Hello."

"What's your name?"

"Tonya."

"Waiting for someone?"

"Yes, my friend Nancy. She'll be here any second."

"Come here often?"

"Sometimes. After work usually."

Without asking, Rory sat down.

"Yeah," he says, nonchalantly, as if I care, "I'm from Seattle and come here after work, too. It's a great place to kick back, have dinner and drinks. Unwind."

Nancy comes through the door. When she sees a man sitting at our table, she scrunches up her face like she has smelled something horrible.

"Oh, here's my friend now," I say, and turn toward her. Rory can't see my face and I blink a couple of times quickly to let her know this is not planned.

After introductions, Nancy sits next to me and Rory tells us all about the football game he was watching before joining us and how he misses Seattle and can't understand the liquor laws here.

Nancy and I do our utmost to be polite but we

came to visit and spend time together. I guess if you are a woman in a restaurant lounge you can expect men to think it is more than just meeting a friend to visit. He excuses himself and goes to the men's room.

"What's he doing here?" Nancy asks, irked.

"He just came over and introduced himself. I couldn't do anything about it."

"Well," she said narrowing her eyes, "if he's a dork I'm getting rid of him."

We are still laughing when he returns. He seems nice enough but I wish Nancy would tell him to leave. After an hour or so, Nancy says she has to go. She is disappointed but needs to get home. Rory asks if I will stay and I decline, telling him I'm stopping at another friends house for a short visit.

"Can I come?" he asks.

Not knowing what to say, I nod my head and say, "sure."

I didn't feel good about him tagging along so I raced my new Jaguar out of the parking lot and screamed up the road hoping to loose him. I cut in and out of traffic and made a sharp turn into Mika's neighborhood. Glancing in the rear view mirror, he is right on my tail. Damn! Stuck.

As usual, Mika and her husband, Rick, are drinking beer and watching television. Rory makes himself comfortable, as if he has known Mika and Rick for a lifetime. I fall asleep on the couch and he stays up all night talking and drinking.

Later, after everyone passed out, I tip-toe out.

Nancy called in the morning to make sure I was all right. "I saw you flying out of the parking lot like you were trying to escape. Are you okay?"

"Yeah, I was stupid enough to invite him to Mika's house but decided I wanted to lose him but couldn't."

We laughed.

Midmorning I get a call from Mika. Rory is still there. He and Rick hit it off and have gone to the liquor store for some Seattle beer.

"He really likes you," Mika tells me.

"So what?" I respond, my hangover making me feel as if I'm on the rolling deck of a ocean going ship.

"I gave him your numbers."

"What! I don't even like the guy. I couldn't lose him last night now you've him my numbers! How could you, Mika."

"He seems okay and he likes you a lot."

"So? I don't give my number to everyone who is interested in me. Get real!"

"He wanted to know all about you," she started. "I told him you weren't looking for anyone right now and that you had a son and owned your own business and . . . "

"You told him all that?" I interrupted. "That's my business . . . How could you, Mika!"

I learned later he spent the entire day at their house and slept on their couch again. Mika got the impression he didn't have a place to go home to; and, that he probably went from one person's living room to the next, camping out.

An hour later, I answer the salon phone and it was Rory.

"Hi Tonya. It's Rory."

"Hi Rory," I say, thinking he has a nice voice.

"Hey, can you meet me for dinner - on me?"

I really didn't know what to say. My mother had Jonny and I was going to go out and eat alone anyway. "Okay. What were you thinking?"

"How about steak or maybe seafood? You pick?"

"Meet me at the salon at eight o'clock."

Rory was right on time. He wanted to go in one car but I insisted he follow me.

"Do you know the Market Street Broiler at the mouth of Big Cottonwood Canyon?" I ask. "The food is fabulous and I'm starving."

"Nope. Never heard of it. This is your town.

You name it and I'll follow you."

Market Street was packed with beautiful women and handsome men; it's an upscale meat market on the weekend. Luckily, we got a booth and Rory ordered expensive wine and wanted to talk about sex. He ogled every woman walking by and commented on how sexy they were. Several times he told me what a fine body I had and he wanted to sit close to me.

I suddenly had a strange feeling about him and was glad we came in separate cars. We ordered steak, crab legs and lobster and another bottle of wine. The food was delicious.

"Boy, that one has such a fine little figure," he said about a young woman who walked by with her date. "The women here are so nice and beautiful, no wonder Ted Bundy liked to come here."

What! I couldn't believe my ears. Ted Bundy? Where did that come from? The way he said it was creepy, like he was whispering and his eyes narrowed and moved from side to side. Not only that, he said he had never heard of the Market Street Grill, how did he know Bundy came here?

When the bill arrived, Rory looked at it and shifted from bun to bun as if the seat was uncomfortable. He gave the waitress a credit card and when the receipt came back he spent a lot of time figuring out the tip and finally signed it.

Just as we were leaving, the waitress came back white as a ghost and nervous.

"I'm sorry sir but you calculated the bill wrong. You wrote down the wrong amount."

"Oh, I did," he said, acting surprised.

He had mistakenly (right!) added incorrectly, reducing the bill by more than one hundred dollars. The waitress stayed at the table as he straightened the mess out. I noticed the manager watching from a doorway not far away.

In the parking lot, he suddenly became very amorous. He wanted to kiss me and hold me tight. His hands were all over me. I pushed him away and he seemed surprised. He wanted to know what was wrong.

"Aren't we going back to your place?" he asked.

"What gave you that idea?"

"Well, the other night with your friend . . . you were so friendly . . . I thought that was what you were there for . . . to pick up a man and take him home . . . for sex."

"I'm sorry you got that impression. That is not what we were doing!"

Leaning towards me, he tried to kiss me. I

moved back and pushed him away. Suddenly, he seemed to change, he was angry and aggressive and I felt frightened. I was glad the parking lot was well lighted and people were around.

"Well," he said in an intense voice, "you know, that was a very expensive dinner, and if we're not going to go to your place, you could at least go half with me."

I reached into my purse as quickly as I could and handed him two one hundred dollar bills.

He smiled when he saw the money, "That should do it!"

I got into my car and hit the door lock. I drove off as quickly as possible. As I left I could see him open the hatch back to his car and climb in over the back seat and into the front. For some reason, he couldn't get the door of his own car to open. As I drove away, I had the real sense that I had just escaped a very ugly situation.

When I got home, I called Nancy and told her what happened. She was glad I was safe and told me that she had had bad feelings about the guy from the beginning.

Chapter Twenty-Two
Family

My flight to the east coast is on the biggest plane I've ever flown on. Three rows and the middle section with seven seats. I'm in the middle row, seat number 10E. Next to me are two young girls about nine or ten. They have headsets on, getting ready for the in-flight movie that won't start until the plane departs. They are more and more antsy with each passing minute. The flight is filled with hyper children and their worn-out parents. Most are returning home from skiing at Utah's premiere resorts.

I don't ski but I have tried it. Once was enough. It took two hours to make it down one hill. Not my idea of a good time. I briefly took up snowboarding after giving Jonny a snowboard for Christmas.

"Come on mom, follow me," he said, sweetly. "You go like this." He showed me how to maneuver down the mountain.

"Hill side, toe side."

"Okay, okay." Some times I would fall and he seemed concerned.

"Are you okay, Mom?"

We did a few runs together, and then he went alone. He is fearless and full of adventure. It was hard for me - his mother - to watch. Instead, I go in the lodge and have a moral beer. What is a moral beer? It's a beer drafted in the only state in the union that's a theocracy. The entire state is run and owned by the Mormon Church.

After becoming airborne, the girl's settle down and watch the movie until the flight attendant delivers dinner. I order a glass of merlot and sit back to mediate on the peace of mind I wish I was experiencing.

"Ma'am," the girl's says in unison.

"Yes, my dear?"

"Would you like some of our dinner?"

"Oh, thank you, but . . . "

"How about the cookies?" one asks, holding the package up.

"Or, how about this cheese?" the other pipes in.

It was Gouda, my favorite. "You are very nice. Thanks, I'll have the cheese."

The girl's mother smiled at their generosity and I thanked them. As I nibbled on the cheese and sipped wine, I remembered Arthur buying Gouda cheese. We went for a small holiday vacation to the sun city of Phoenix for New Years. He has purchased some rental properties in the area - and he ultimately wants to relocate there - and he has a place where we sat on the patio and drank wine and enjoyed Gouda. It was most enchanting.

"Shall we go to the jazz club?" he asks. "Some place I can enjoy a cigar?"

"Sure, why not."

We climb into his XJ8 Jaguar and blast off. I call it the old and powerful man's car. It suits him.

The Jazz club is half filled and everyone is coupled up. The band is playing songs from Frank Sinatra, Dean Martin and old blue eyes himself, Bing Crosby.

"Could I get a Scotch on the rocks with a splash of water?"

"And for you?" The waitress asks.

" I'll have a Cosmopolitan."

The band consists of a piano player, singer and a small horn section.

Arthur lights up his cigar, sits back and enjoys the music. It was written all over his face, "This is the life!"

We could never do this in Utah. It is the only place I know of where you can buy a cigar at a cigar shop, but you can't smoke it there. Then, of course, we get the sin tax. It is their way of collecting money we hadn't given to the church as tithing.

It is difficult for Arthur - for many people - to live in such an ill-fitting place as Utah. Personal choice to do what one wishes is often supplanted by right-wing ultra conservative lawmakers, who believe we all would be better off if we were more like them: bored stiff and bursting with hypocrisy.

"Can I have some of your Cosmo?" Arthur asks.

"Of course."

We enjoyed the music and he savored his cigar and then went home. As we drove, his hands were all over me. There is nothing quite as wonderful as the warmth of a man's hands holding and caressing your body. I really love it when Arthur holds my hand; his hands surrounds mine in a protective way. I feel safe and warm and content.

"I can't wait to get you home," he says.

I knew what I was in for. We hadn't really been alone for weeks. Arthur is a very passionate man. His need for lovemaking is intense. And, it's not that I don't enjoy it, I do, but sometimes the anticipation is more fun than the act for me.

At his place, the heat of passion flowed through my body. He takes over and I wonder if it is never going to end. Although he pleases himself - really satiates himself - he always makes sure everything is as good for me. Few men are as thoughtful, at least not in my past relationships.

At the Richmond, Virginia airport I notice a group of black men standing along the concourse eyeing me up and down. I smile at them and they look away - embarrassed. Haven't they ever seen a red head in a short skirt and stiletto's before? After the shock of me smiling sunk in, several tip their head respectfully and smile back. The airport is filled with people of every color and culture. Airports are the crossroads of life, places where we all come together with a common goal - to get back home. Living in a mono-culture like Utah one seldom sees as many people of color.

Virginia is beautiful, lush with trees and bushes and forests. The people seem open and friendly and more willing to accept others.

Back on the plane, I remember coming home from my grandparents as a five-year-old. My special stewardess - that's what they were called back then - was a tall, thin, beautiful chocolate colored woman named Betty. She took care of me and made me laugh. In Salt Lake City, she escorted me to my parents, who were waiting. As I turned to tell her good bye, I said, "Bye, Black Betty." She just smiled and laughed. My parents were very embarrassed but they hoped she understood. I'm sure she did.

I have never been anyone's wife, but I have

been called "a wife" once in a while. Recently, I helped a friend who was an exhibitor at a local tradeshow. I helped greet people at her booth and do whatever I could. Arthur stopped by and while visiting spotted a couple from a distance, "Hey, I think I know that woman from somewhere."

I wonder, is it from a strip club? She was a bottle blonde and anorexic-looking: young, tall, thin, long hair and tons of make-up. I kept my mouth shut.

When they arrived at my friend's booth, the young woman recognized Arthur but neither could put a finger on who the other person was, or where they knew each other from.

The woman hands him her business card and, in turn, he reached into his pocket but could not find one of his cards. Turning to me, he asks, "Honey, do you have any of my cards?"

"Sorry, no."

Arthur gives her one of my cards and writes his telephone number on the back.

She takes the card, and says, "Here is an extra card for your wife."

After she leaves, Arthur shakes his head and says, "Boy, that is weird."

"What?"

"Jonny called me Dad the other day and now

you've been called my wife! Strange, isn't it? How do you feel about being called my wife?"

"I don't know. I have never been a wife before. So, I don't know what it is suppose to feel like."

Arthur has been a husband twice but never a father. When Jonny called him dad he was pleasantly surprised.

We had just left the house, on our way to dinner. Nothing fancy, just some real food. Making dinner at home is turning into the luxury that going out to eat once was. Going out to dinner is the norm now, a replacement for the home cooked meal.

"Jonny," I enquired, "did you change the sheets on your bed?"

"No."

"Why not?"

"I don't know."

I have been after Jonny to take responsibility for cleaning his room and change his sheets. At least two weeks had elapsed since I requested he change his sheets. I could easily see the sheets were filthy but he was sleeping in them and I figured he would get tired of it and change them. For my part, I simply was getting to the point of being just too tired to care.

How does one maintain a household on one

income, run a business, and travel around the country representing another company without losing one's mind? I have to pay all my expenses plus all of those from my salon. Every morning I have to chase Jonny out of the house and off to school. It is always a fight. Having him help me around the house by cleaning his own room seems reasonable to me. But, like most teenaged boys, Jonny seems allergic to even cleaning up after himself.

Two weeks early, when I insisted he change his sheets he had gotten sick with the stomach flu and had an accident in his bed. When I got home he seemed better but there was a stain on one of his sheet.

"What is that?" I asked.

"Oh, that was from when I was sick."

"Well, don't you think you should change your sheets?"

"No, you do it Mom."

"You know Jonny, one day I am not going to be around to do everything for you. Who do you think is going to clean up after you? Do you Laundry? Fold your clothes?"

"I don't know."

As he sits at his little desk, half naked in his boxer shorts, playing computer games, I can see he is just a child. The computer games have created an uncomfortable looking lazy belly. He's getting a bit fat for his age and I am sure the computer and the endless snacks are the reason.

Arthur who is driving, asks, "Why does he need to change his sheets?"

"Well, don't you like a fresh pair of sheets at least once a week? I know I do."

I didn't want to embarrass Jonny by telling Arthur that Jonny had spoiled the sheets - that he was sleeping in his own shit - but I'm not a good liar and the truth came out.

"You have got to be kidding!" Arthur exclaimed, horrified. Turning to Jonny, he asks, "You have been sleeping in your own shit for over two weeks now?"

Silence.

"That is just sick! Is it because you are too lazy to change your sheets?"

No answer.

"Well, you are going to change them when we get home."

"No, I'm not."

"Yes, you are."

Jonny mouthed a swear word under his breath. In one gesture, Arthur reached into the back seat and smacked him, "You can mouth off to your mother all you want but I won't let you disrespect me!"

I was secretly glad Arthur had taken charge. I am sometimes too tired to argue.

"Fine," Jonny said, as we pull into the restaurant parking lot. "I'm not going in."

"Then don't." Arthur replied.

I opened the car door and Jonny slowly followed. We were both worried he was going to pout and act like a baby. He didn't. I think he needed someone to tell him to stop being disrespectful.

Later, at home while I was on the phone trying to fix Jonny's internet connection, Arthur and Jonny changed the sheets and cleaned up his room.

"Now see, Jonny," Arthur said, "that wasn't that hard. Why don't you do things to help your Mom? Your really just helping yourself. She is sitting on the phone, fixing your internet and you should do something for her."

I think they secretly like each other. I sometimes get in the way.

"Okay, your internet is fixed," I tell him, standing in the doorway. "I'm going to go unpack my bag."

While I unpacked, Arthur went to check on Jonny. Unbeknownst to Jonny, Arthur was standing in the doorway as he was talking on the speaker phone to a friend.

"What are you doing?" the caller asked.

"Cleaning my room for my Mom and Dad."

"Only pussies do what their parents want them to do."

Outraged, Arthur shouted back, "Oh really, then get your pussy ass over here and help him."

Surprised, Jonny jumped up and out of his chair. He quickly hit the speaker button so Arthur couldn't hear the conversation.

"Okay," Arthur said, "I just wanted to make sure you kept up the good work." He turned and left.

Arthur told me about the incident. We laughed.

"I can't believe it."

"What?"

"These kids talk back and forth as if doing something for your parents makes you pussy-whipped. I haven't heard that since I was in high school." He repeated it, "Pussy-whipped. That gives me a whole new idea on what these kids are thinking and why they are so lazy."

Arthur paused and seemed thoughtful, "Jonny called me Dad to his friend. Weird."

I secretly think he liked being called Dad. I could see it in the twinkle of his eye, like Santa Claus.

Chapter Twenty-Three
Arthur in Phoenix

Arthur is in the sun city of the Phoenix, working his new business venture. He sold his salon, let his clients go, gathered all his resources, found investors and bought an apartment complex in Phoenix. He's turning the apartments into condos. He is spending half of his time there and half here. Soon, he will cut all ties here and leave this Taliban-style, religious capitol of western America. His courage and determination is admirable and enviable. I can't help but feel weak and indecisive around a man like this.

I knew the time would come when he would leave - and once again I would be left alone. But, it's different this time, I am older and not the child of despair I once was. Arthur continues to reinforce the idea of us remaining together and has encouraged me to sell off everything and join him. One voice in me says go; another says, wait and see.

I haven't called him because lately I feel my calls annoy him. Once, not so long ago, he longed to hear my voice any time of day or night. Now, I feel as if I am intruding and he doesn't have the time or inclination for me. I remember when he would call just to hear my voice. Now, I sense he is not listening when we talk.

Airport

I am standing at the curb outside Sky Harbor Airport in Phoenix, waiting to be reunited with Arthur. I have two carry-on bags filled with lingerie; I intend to leave several of his favorite pieces laying around so he can be reminded that I am his when I am gone.

Here he comes, driving his big powerful jaguar. I can see his furrowed brow and frustration even at this distance. I have seen this look before. He is what he is, all grumpy and powerful. This is part of the skin of his new business endeavor. His soul is awakening to the vibrancy that resides in his eyes.

Arthur's face softens when he finally sees me. His eyes fill with a lusty glaze, his smile turns up at the corners. Out of the car, he takes me into his arms. Oh, oh! The warmth of his lips against mine; our passion collides and our bodies press and mingle together. We are whole once more. All the anguish and pain of the separation has evaporated.

Pulling away from the curb his real mood resurfaces.

"Fuck!" he shouts, "Damn it!"

"What?" His voice frightens me.

"I do this every time I pick you up!"

"What?" I look from side to side to see what he is talking about.

I am stunned at his angry tone. "What's wrong?"

"I can't seem to ever take the right exit out of here! I always end up clear the fuck over here."

"That's a problem?" It wasn't as if we had made an enormous mistake. I could tell he had had a long day. He always gets antsy when he makes mistakes.

He glances at me and laughs. Arthur always laughs when he is nervous, uncomfortable or angry. It doesn't stop his anger but it somehow disarms the situation.

For a moment, I have the nagging fear he doesn't want me here.

Once out of the airport, we start making out. His hands are all over me. He wants to get me home as quickly as possible. Lovemaking helps keep him grounded and it brings us together.

At his new bachelor pad, we can't decide whether to sit on the patio and enjoy a glass of wine first or get down to business in the bedroom. We compromise and take the wine into the bed.

After sex, I profess my love for him. I pour my heart out and gush with love like a teenager.

"Suck up," he calls out, and blows a kiss to me.

Oh, how I love this man! He pulls me down on

top of him again. Ecstasy.

Later, we dress and go to a nightclub he frequents. After enjoying a drink, he says he'll be right back and disappears. Twenty minutes later he is still missing. I see him going from the bar to different tables, from one woman to another, talking and flirting. He seems to think I enjoy watching him search for other women. Am I not good enough for him?

Wendy, our server, tells me it's last call and I look for Arthur but he has disappeared.

"Oh, bring us two, I guess." I answer.

After a few minutes, I see him sitting at a table across the room with an anorexic bottle blonde. She has the biggest implants on the planet.

Am I not getting the memo? Where do I stand, or do I stand at all? Fucked again! Maybe he is bored and needs the thrill of finding someone new.

I suddenly wish I was home in my wonderful house, alone with a big glass of wine. I would stand naked in front of the full length mirror and admire myself. I want to be loved and accepted for who I am. I do not want to wear make-up or do my hair. I want someone to really love me just as I am. Who am I?

Chapter Twenty-Four
Fate

As fate is once again before me, I can only wait for the departure of my next flight. I have a choice to make. A choice to stay or leave. I can stay in my luxury home with everything it has taken years to acquire or I can sell it all including my business and move to Arizona to be with Arthur. I know this decision will take courage but it has more to do with trust than with anything else.

It is not just about trusting Arthur, which is an enormous gamble, but about trusting my own judgment. I have made good calls, and an equal number of bad ones. Love has such great allure. Love and true companionship could be the deepest currents in the ocean of our soul. It is something none of us takes lightly and yet, my heart speaks with one voice - and reality and logic with another.

Am I willing to give up the safe and comfortable fortress I have created for my son and myself for the beckoning unknown? I think of the old Russian proverb, "Fool me once, shame on you. Fool me twice, shame on me." I have trusted my heart and the vagaries of love many times and they have blinded me to reality. Is it happening again? Is love just a game of Tom-foolery we play on ourselves? Do we trick ourselves into believing we might obtain our fairytale love?

Every time I escape a bad relationship, I am surprised by how suddenly clarity and focus return. The blind spots evaporate and the truth stands out like the Statue of Liberty, clear and resounding. My prince charming turns out to be boys or little men who cheat and lie. If one of my best friends were dating any of these men, I would tell her to run - not walk - to the nearest exit.

Despite my mistakes and missteps, there is something about love that keeps me searching. I feel desperate to find a forever home and security. It makes good sense that I search for love but it renders me unable to see clearly; we all seem to ignore or discount all warning signs and hard evidence that don't jive with our desires and we exaggerate the smallest or most insignificant pluses, making them more important than they truly are.

Arthur has been hurt by love, too. He is deeply sensitive and fearful I will do to him what his wives did. He worries he should be doing more for me and he tries so hard to make sure he doesn't take over or impose himself in my decisions. He admires me; I see it in his face and in his actions. He trusts my judgment and gives me an equal place in all discussions and shared concerns. He is a mans-man but has the tender heart of a man raised by a loving woman. He will protect and take care of me even though I am independent and stand on my own stilettos. Arthur is the man I have been waiting for, someone who accepts me for who and what I am. Someone who loves me - with or without makeup. He never holds back. I know he loves me.

Will I leave my fortress - the fabulous house and patio and swimming pool; the ever failing to thrive business that despite its problems has given me an excellent income; the always complaining women clients who are never satisfied but who dish out big money for my services; the high paying primetime consulting job that takes me away to exciting destinations and values my beauty; the expensive European convertibles of my choice; the valued friends and associates that has taken a lifetime to acquire - so Arthur can break my heart and leave me for an anorexic, tits on a stick, bottle blonde?

Yes! This time I know my man truly loves me. He wants to kiss me every morning, noon and night. He teases me if I forget to kiss him hello and goodbye. He watches me when he thinks I don't notice; he adores me. When he knows I am running low on my favorite wine he stops and gets more. When he see me struggle, he stands next to me and lends his strength. He would fight my battles and go down for me.

Yes! A thousand times YES! I will go anywhere and do anything for this man. He has given me the fairytale love I have so long desired, so long dreamed about. The little girl in me who nearly lost her life sleigh riding sings joyously deep within when I am with him. He is my Christopher, the horse, carrying me on his strong back and protecting me.

Who knows what tomorrow brings. It could all come tumbling down around my shoulders - but if it does, I have known a true love. So, let the day bring on the night and let the night be followed by the dawn of each new day. I rejoice.

I am finally at peace.

Printed in the United States
200176BV00001B/1-117/A

9 780977 042456